Spirituality, Evolution & Awakened Consciousness

*Getting Real About Soul Maturity
and Spiritual Growth*

Insight & Awareness books and courses are maps that assist you with your evolution and the process of soul recovery.

A map only becomes useful if you are willing to use it as a guide.
Life is a journey of self-discovery.
As you trek along your own path with self-awareness,
you begin to see there is a bigger picture.

Insight & Awareness books and courses are maps that help you
navigate the complexities of yourself.
They also enable you to develop new perspectives on the significance of
where you have been,
where you are now,
and where you can choose to go.
A map is a tool for an explorer that highlights
what to look for during their expedition.
Are you a spiritual explorer?

Understanding your life experience and your emotions
Insight & Awareness

Lorraine Nilon is a Soul Intuitive®, Insightful Life Coach, Philosopher and Spiritual Teacher. She is the creator of Insight & Awareness, which offers books, online courses, workshops, intensive retreats, and private sessions. Her life purpose is to teach others about the importance of self-reflection and soul exploration.

Lorraine explains the merits of discovering the parts of us that cause us to be disconnected from the truth of who we naturally are. She is a spiritual tour guide for those who want to get real about themselves and are willing to embrace the uniqueness of their soul journey.

She is an advocate for feet-on-the-ground spirituality and has a way of sparking your curiosity, which is a precursor to reconnecting to the meaningfulness of your own existence, recovering from the wounds you carry and rejuvenating the way you interact with life.

All the books in the Insight and Awareness Anthology and courses expose the labyrinth of our life experiences, emotions, and soul truth. They highlight the hidden lessons and are designed to assist you on your individual journey. It is easy to get lost, to give up, or to deny the significance of your evolutionary path. These books and courses are reminders that you are worth the required effort.

Insight & Awareness
Books and courses for your soul!

FREE e-book available @ www.Lorraine Nilon.com.au

Take a Moment to Reflect

Contemplation Nurtures your Soul

Also available FREE 12-day emailed Companion Contemplation Course.

Improve your self-reflection skills.

Free download

Take a Moment to Reflect
Contemplation Nurtures Your Soul

As a bonus for purchasing an Insight & Awareness book,
go to Lorraine's website to receive your free e-book copy of
Take a Moment to Reflect

www.lorrainenilon.com.au

Spirituality, Evolution & Awakened Consciousness

Getting Real About Soul Maturity
and Spiritual Growth

LORRAINE NILON

Illustrations by Katherine Close

Understanding your life experience
and your emotions

Insight &
Awareness

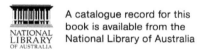

NATIONAL LIBRARY OF AUSTRALIA

A catalogue record for this book is available from the National Library of Australia

Author: Nilon, Lorraine Dawn.
Title: Spirituality, Evolution & Awakened Consciousness
Illustrator: Katherine Close

ISBN: 978-0-6488694-0-5 (Softcover)
ISBN: 978-0-6488694-1-2 (Hardcover)
ISBN: 978-0-6488694-2-9 (E-book)

Illustrations and book cover by Katherine Close

Understanding your life experience and your emotions

Insight & Awareness

You have the freedom to determine the path of your soul journey.

**Dedicated to the spiritual explorers
who feel compelled to ask questions and
are inspired to follow where their questions lead them.**

**May this book be a reminder that your soul journey is a
wondrous, significant adventure.**

Life is unpredictable and our personal currents takes us where we need to go.

The intention of this book is to heighten your awareness of:

- The intricacy of being a soul.
- How life is a process of self-discovery.
- The value of exploring your spirituality.
- The significance of understanding yourself.
- The importance of being real and grounded in your quest to understand spirituality.

Contents

Section 3

Section 4

Section 5

Our soul's unconsciousness - emotional baggage - can become very messy as we gather and store what we refuse to acknowledge and deal with truthfully. Life is an opportunity to resolve what burdens our souls, so we can evolve into the authenticity of who we naturally are.

Preface

To understand the true meaning of spirituality, evolution and awakened consciousness, we have to acknowledge the complexity of who we are. We are all souls sharing the experience of life within a physical body. How we approach this experience has a huge impact on the way we live, and on the legacy we leave our souls to carry.

We are an interface—the point where two systems meet and interact. We are the connection point between our origins and life on earth, also between consciousness and unconsciousness. Being a connection point between two worlds has been part of the mysteries of life and may remain so until we return to our origins. However, in the meantime, we are living a life where we get to choose the type of energy we create and contribute to our world.

We have freewill, and the energy of our soul's consciousness and unconsciousness are constantly putting us in a position of choice. We may not be aware of these choices, but we still make them. The majority of the time we react unconsciously. Being aware—conscious—occurs through the intent to be so. Life is the arena of freewill, and we navigate our experiences with the choices we make. We either choose to feed the consciousness or the unconsciousness of our earthly soul system. This is simplifying it, as we are complex human beings. The decisions we make reflect the types of energy we value, our intent, and how far we are willing to separate from the truth of our souls.

We get to decide if we produce and project more unconscious energy into the world we live in, or if we are going to be a source of conscious energy. Understanding the truth of the energy we align with, nurture, and project into the world requires us to understand ourselves, and that is spirituality.

When we acknowledge we are the interface between our own soul's consciousness and unconsciousness, we realise we have an opportunity to evolve. Recognising this and taking responsibility for being the pivotal point in our own evolutionary journey makes a difference in how we interact with life.

Our soul's unconsciousness is the storehouse of our emotional baggage, and we keep creating more unconscious energy to store. The rules of freewill allow us to carry this energy, lifetime after lifetime. We carry the unconscious energy of our own making until we are ready to confront the truth of ourselves and engage with the process of resolving what we've created that burdens our souls.

We can choose to confront ourselves and deal with the energies we have stored in our soul's unconsciousness. We can use our truthfulness to resolve and convert the unconscious energy into conscious understanding. This process of changing energy and, expanding our awareness and self-knowledge is evolution. Evolution is the process of developing changes that create emotional growth and soul maturity.

Evolution is the process of evolving from a primitive state to the more advanced one of unifying with the truth of our souls. However, to do this, we have to resolve the energy produced by our beliefs, fears, and barriers to truth, because we use these to uphold our framework of soul oppression. This leaves us protecting our avenues of indifference to truth. These avenues are sequenced patterns that cause us to stay on an emotional merry-go-round, acting out what we refuse to acknowledge or deal with. Our own indifference to truth often causes us to succumb to the seven deadly sins in an attempt to fill the internal void we feel. This void is created as we separate from our awareness of our own soul.

Evolution is not easy, nor is it impossible, but it does require us to be present and aware of ourselves and reality. The key is being truthful with ourselves. This book is a way of starting a conversation with yourself about how you want to live and interact with your own soul.

Our unconsciousness is a type of labyrinth that is at times difficult to navigate. Just when you think you have it sorted, there is another layer to the labyrinth. Labyrinths are considered easy to walk—just follow the path to the centre, and from there the path will return you to the same entry point. We make the labyrinth difficult, and it is the resolution of how we make it a complex, convoluted web of unconscious energy that enables us to unify with the truth of our souls. When we front up, accept the journey and trust the significance of our souls, the labyrinth becomes an adventure to unburden our souls.

Life is also a labyrinth: We enter a physical body, walk the passageways of life, and our various experiences enable us to encounter the diversity of energy within our souls. We exit the physical body at the end of our lifetime.

Awakened consciousness is unification within ourselves, with reality and our origins. Understanding the truth of this requires a journey of self-discovery. We have to walk the labyrinths we encounter, comprehend them, learn the lessons, then walk it again to see if we've retained and are willing to use our new knowledge.

Spirituality, Evolution & Awakened Consciousness is a reminder to contemplate the significance of your own spirituality, evolution and awakening consciousness. Don't just see these as words or concepts to toss around. Align with your internal yearning to truly comprehend what they mean to you. This book will not have all the answers you seek, although I hope it ignites your curiosity. It will invoke questions within you that enable you to trust life as an expedition, encouraging you to become a fellow explorer—an explorer who seeks unification with truth and feet-on-the-ground spirituality. One who values being aware of reality, wants to be of truth, embraces uniqueness and is willing to get real and apply effort to unify all the fragmented aspects of your soul.

This book is an expedition to reconnect with your own insight and awareness.

Throughout the book, you may find it beneficial to refer to the glossary for an explanation of the unique terminology used. It's also helpful to familiarise yourself with the different aspects of your soul system. For more information see – An Overview of Your Energetic System.

When we mindfully explore the labyrinth of life,
we evolve through our discoveries.
When we refuse to acknowledge the opportunities life presents,
we become stuck in the labyrinth, unaware that we are the key to unburdening our souls.

Contemplation

Give yourself time to contemplate how you feel about what you are reading and take notice of your thoughts and reactions. Allow yourself a moment to recognise and accept the truth of your feelings. Acknowledge your own awareness, resonance with truth, and internal knowing. Embrace your curiosity.

Let this book be a contemplation adventure.

1. Some statements are numbered. Pick one and take the time to contemplate it.

2. If a sentence, concept, or illustration stands out to you, openly discuss it with others and accept there will be varying views.

3. Try journaling about a sentence, quote, paragraph, concept, chapter, or illustration. Whatever you want to contemplate.

   Come back to what you have journaled about later, without reading the previous entry and after familiarising yourself with the same sentence, quote, paragraph, concept, chapter or illustration in this book, journal again.

   Then compare, so you can recognise and unravel your own insight and awareness.

When you see ...., this is an invitation to add your views. Your opinions matter! They are expressions of your thoughts, beliefs, and logic. They may be a starting point for further exploration. As your awareness expands, your opinions can change, become reaffirmed, or are completely discarded. Sometimes you have to acknowledge when an opinion is outdated and no longer represents you. You may realise it was never your opinion, only a hangover from what you had been indoctrinated to believe.

It is important to give yourself time to contemplate what you are reading, as it allows you to absorb what resonates with you. It also helps you to challenge yourself about your own insight and awareness.

Contemplation cultivates an inner connection, an awareness of yourself.
I don't mean your emotional self; I mean the part of you hidden beneath your emotional baggage—your soul's consciousness.

Your soul's consciousness is the part of you that has never abandoned the unconditional love of your origins or your awareness of truth. Your soul's consciousness is the truth of who you are and the natural core of your being.

Contemplation and self-reflection seem to be skills we are losing. We live in a world of instant gratification, addicted to using screens to occupy our minds. We are becoming less observant and more entrenched in our judgement, because we are bombarded with the same views and opinions.

We rant and rave, but seem less likely to thoughtfully contemplate all aspects and examine the truth we feel. We do not acknowledge our internal reality. We compare ourselves to others' social media images, and many of us feel left behind and not good enough. We are being sold a story that notoriety equates to contentment, but most feel frustrated and disconnected.

We are losing our ability to learn from ourselves, to put events in perspective and to expand our own awareness. We are losing the art of being self-inspiring.

Contemplation information is an excerpt from another title from the Insight and Awareness Anthology—
Lorraine Nilon.
Energy of Souls - Understanding Your Soul System to Expand Your Emotional and Spiritual Maturity.

True Source Divine Origin Consciousness

Your Soul's Consciousness

We are a dichotomy of
consciousness and unconsciousness.
Our soul's consciousness is the purity
of our soul and is always connected
to the truth of our origins.
Our soul's unconsciousness is the
storehouse of our emotional baggage.
It is the result of our denial of our
soul and of the significance of truth.

Your Soul's Unconsciousness

Soul Denial

Overview of Your Energetic System

This is a brief overview of the energetic systems of souls on Earth. It will help you understand the concepts explored in this book and in other titles from the Insight and Awareness Anthology. If you are interested in a deeper exploration of the energetics, *Energy of Souls* and *Your Insight and Awareness Book* may interest you.

Different labels can be used to mean the same thing, but they are only labels. Beneath each label is an essence. The essence is what we learn from and resonate with. The following are the terminology used in the Insight and Awareness Anthology. *True Source Divine Origin Consciousness* is also known as Universe, God or Great Spirit. Use whatever term you feel comfortable with. Regardless of the terminology each of us is used to or prefer to use, the process of understanding is the same.

True Source Divine Origin Consciousness is a label for the collective purity of truth and is the collective energy of the truth of all souls and the origin of your soul. This is where you come from and where you will return to after your death. This label is used because you do not have a history with it. It is a way of counteracting what you believe you know and enables you to have the freedom to explore your own discovery about your origin of truth. *True Source Divine Origin Consciousness* is the source of your soul's consciousness.

True Source Divine Origin Consciousness has been written in italics to emphasise the significance of truth. The italics are a way of drawing your attention to the importance of your origin of truth. It is also a reminder that you are not alone on your soul journey. *True Source Divine Origin Consciousness* is present and can be felt in your truthfulness and your recognition of your soul.

Your soul's consciousness is the part of you that has never abandoned the unconditional love of your origins or your awareness of truth. Your soul's consciousness is the truth of who you are and is naturally the core of your being. It is the purity of your soul.

You are the interface between your soul's consciousness and unconsciousness.

Your soul truth is the reality of both the conscious energy of your consciousness and the unconscious energy of your soul's unconsciousness.

Core essences are unique strands of conscious energy that are part of the purity of who you are. They are the unique strands of conscious energy within *unconditional love*. Core essences are natural energies that emanate from your soul's consciousness.

Here is a list of the core essences explored from different angles in the Insight and Awareness Anthology. There are many more and you may want to add to the list.

- *Acceptance*
- *Appreciation*
- *Care*
- *Clarity*
- *Compassion*
- *Dynamism*
- *Freedom*
- *Grace*
- *Harmony*

- *Honesty*
- *Hope*
- *Independence*
- *Individuality*
- *Integrity*
- *Joy*
- *Kindness*
- *Loyalty*
- *Patience*

- *Peace*
- *Purity*
- *Serenity*
- *Trust*
- *Truthfulness*
- *Uniqueness*
- …………….
- …………….
- …………….

Feelings are the truth we feel. They originate from our soul's consciousness—the core of your being—and there is an intuitive knowing intermingled with the feeling. It is often a hidden awareness of our soul perception. Feelings flow and are an expression of our recognition of our own presence, in relation to the truth we are experiencing.

When feelings are suppressed and ignored, we morph them into emotions. If left unaddressed they become carried unresolved emotions—they may differ from the original feeling, as we ignorantly or arrogantly oppose the truth we feel.

Emotions are an expression of our emotional reactiveness. They stem from what we've stored and continue to carry in our soul's unconsciousness. They are steered by, and entwined with our wants, expectations, beliefs and control structures. Many of which originate from a rejection of our feelings and awareness of truth.

Emotions are stagnant and remain unaddressed until consciously acknowledged. They create and become the fuel that sustain our merry-go-round of soul-oppressive energy—emotional cyclic patterns—that leave us stuck in our unconsciousness. Emotions power repressive thoughts and false negative self-beliefs.

We are at our best when we are of our core essences.

Your soul's unconsciousness is the part of your soul system that is unconscious to the unconditional love of *True Source Divine Origin Consciousness*. It is your emotional baggage. Your soul's unconsciousness is the energetic storehouse of your unconscious energy.

Your soul's unconsciousness consists of your:

- Soul-denial
- Fears
- Embedded beliefs
- Unresolved emotions
- Barriers to truth
- Control structures
- Framework of soul oppression
- The energy of the seven deadly sins

You create, invoke, and sustain the energy of your soul's unconsciousness and use it to deny the truth of who you are. Resolution of your soul's unconsciousness is essential for the evolution of your soul.

Your soul-denial is the crux of your soul's unconsciousness and the source of all unconscious energy. Your soul-denial is generated from your war with the truth of who you are, which enslaves you to exist within the unconsciousness of your soul. Your soul-denial consists of your embedded beliefs and fears, which inhibit you from accepting your natural significance, uniqueness, independence, and individuality. They are also the gateway for you, to operate from the seven deadly sins.

There are many aspects of the energetic vortex of our soul's unconsciousness that we use to imprison ourselves. It requires us to truly care for our own soul and to resolve what we have stored or are willing to create and utilise that sustains our emotional and energetic prison.

Spirituality is the journey to understand all aspects of our soul's consciousness and unconsciousness. Evolution is to learn, grow, and evolve with awareness and understanding.

Awakened consciousness is to flow, unified with the purity of your soul and the divinity of your origins.

True Source Divine Origin Consciousness

Your Soul's Consciousness

Heresy - Desire to control, indifference to truth, resentment of reality, oppositional energy, programming, conditioning and indoctrinations, guilt, shame, humiliation, denial of reality, disassociation from feeling

Controlled evolution - desire to control your soul denial with beliefs.

Images, illusions and controled identities.

Framework
of
Soul
Oppression

Judgement, manipulation, confusion and control

Barriers to Truth

Resistance, denial, avoidance and co-dependency.

Illusion
of control

Desire
to control

Soul Denial
Embedded Beliefs and Fears

Fears come in two types: One reminds you to be alert within your present moment. It's a warning signal from your soul's consciousness, to acknowledge what you feel, recognise the danger of a situation, and trust your insight and awareness.

The other is a negative energy you generate with your thoughts that may or may not be related to the truth of your reality. You generate this sensation of fear from your soul's unconsciousness, and it stems from your desire to avoid or control truth. These fears are often entwined with embedded beliefs or are a direct result of your anxiety about experiencing:

- Distress
- Control failure
- Others' judgement
- A reaction to the unknown
- A reoccurrence of something you know hurts
- Acknowledge what your personal views are ....

Embedded beliefs are opinions, attitudes, and ideals you regard as relevant or true. They are thoughts and emotions that merge to create a philosophy you believe is good judgement. These are deeply fixed in the crux of your soul's unconsciousness—soul-denial. They are integrated into how you perceive yourself, others, life, and truth. These beliefs are surrounded by reinforcing energies, such as fear, denial, and indifference to truth. Embedded beliefs become ways of thinking—mentalities—that inhibit your awareness of truth and sustain your own soul oppression.

Your unresolved emotions are what you use to energetically sustain the vortex of your soul's unconsciousness. These are the emotions you refuse to resolve or are so unconscious of that you deny their existence. All unresolved emotions are unconscious energy. There are many reasons why you have unresolved emotions; however, they are sustained by your fear, and your inability or unwillingness, to face the truth. Some unresolved emotions are a direct result of your dishonesty with yourself.

Control structures are complex methods and mythologies of how you utilise your desire for control or your illusion of having control. Control structures can become very complex systems that sustain your emotional, energetic, and physical barriers to truth. They also strengthen your avenues of indifference within your framework of soul oppression.

Framework of soul oppression consists of your various avenues of indifference, which are sequenced reactions and responses that you use to remain indifferent to truth. These avenues of indifference originate from the fears and embedded beliefs within your soul-denial.

As we trigger the emotional sequenced cycle of soul oppression, our indifference energy ascends from our soul-denial to our heresy barrier, and it descends back to our soul-denial. The indifference energy is fuelled by our soul control, which is our desire for control and our illusion of control.

The avenues of indifference are:

- **Soul abuse:** stems from a willingness to ritualistically hurt yourself or others. Cyclic patterns of pain, hurt, and wounds.

- **Soul betrayal:** stems from deliberate acts of self-disloyalty and the willingness to destroy your trust in others or their trust in you. Cyclic patterns of trauma, deliberate disloyalty, and violation.

- **Soul control:** stems from your desire for control and your illusion of having control. Cyclic patterns of attempted dominance or feeling obsessed and frustrated.

- **Soul deception:** stems from the willingness to mislead yourself and others. Cyclic patterns of torment, exploitation, and manipulation.

- **Soul defiance:** stems from resisting and devaluing truth. Cyclic patterns of opposition, insolence, and judgement.

- **Soul demise:** stems from losing awareness of your soul's consciousness and disregarding your own intuition. Cyclic patterns of feigned forgetfulness or disassociation from both your internal and external world.

- **Soul denial:** stems from your rejection of the significance of being a soul. Cyclic patterns of self-rejection, contradiction, and disconnection.

- **Soul illusion:** stems from the narratives you tell yourself and the portrayed images you use to override your internal knowing or to avoid self-responsibility. Cyclic patterns of pretence, delusion, and confabulation.

- **Soul sabotage:** stems from your willingness to align with any actions, beliefs, energies, and fears you know will heighten your ability to disrupt and impair your natural value, worth, and significance. Cyclic patterns of disruption, harm, and self-perpetuated obstacles.

- **Soul traitor:** stems from the deliberate oppressing of your authentic self or another authenticity. Cyclic patterns of distrust, conspiracy, and dumbing yourself down.

These emotional patterns generate the energy you use to oppress the truth of yourself.

True Source Divine Origin Consciousness

Your Soul's Consciousness

Heresy

Desire to control, indifference to truth, resentment of reality, oppositional energy, programming, conditioning and indoctrinations, guilt, shame, humiliation, denial of reality, Disassociation from feeling love.

Controlled evolution - desire to control your soul denial with beliefs.

Images, illusions and controlled identities.

Judgement, manipulation, confusion and control.

Resistance, denial, avoidance and co-dependency.

Soul Denial

Barriers to truth are energies you use to maintain your separation from your awareness of your soul. Barriers are part of the energetic structural web of the vortex of your soul's unconsciousness. They are sustained by energies that oppose truth and they serve as our defence mechanisms.

The barriers are:

- Resistance, denial, avoidance, and codependency.

- Judgement, manipulation, confusion, and control.

- Images, illusions and controlled identities—roles we use as self-definitions.

- Controlled evolution is the energy within beliefs and narratives that force you to remain stagnant in the evolving process. It also stems from the belief that you are able to control the energy of your soul's unconsciousness to provide you with what you believe will quell the inner confusion, fill the void you feel, or protect your other barriers to truth.

- Heresy is the energy used to remain indifferent towards the truth of your own actions, which results in you being anti-truth and anti-yourself. Heresy is a barrier that consists of many unconscious energies:

  Your desire for control, indifference to truth, resentment of reality, and willingness to be oppositional to whatever challenges your narrative and embedded beliefs.

  Your programming, conditioning, and indoctrinations are filters that distort your perception and suffocate your ability to learn and evolve.

  Guilt, shame, humiliation, and denial of reality become the go-to positions, stifling your own self-acceptance.

  The energies of the heresy barrier result in disassociating from self-love.

Barriers are control structures formed from your layers of triggered emotional reactions. They sustain your deception and prevent your awareness of the flow of truth within you. They inhibit your ability to recognise and learn from the truth of your reality.

Seven deadly sins are forms of indifference that have plagued mankind. These energies reinforce the unconscious energy within your soul's unconsciousness, and they leave you operating from compulsion. This leads you to be indifferent to yourself and truth. The use of any of the seven deadly sins, singularly or in any combination, invokes false promises. They are transgressions that are fatal to your participation in your evolution, as you become seduced by your own indifference to truth.

The seven deadly sins are lust, greed, gluttony, envy, sloth, wrath, and pride:

- **Lust** is to covet and crave possessing control of another person or something—it is a desire for the power to take without giving back.

- **Greed** is the desire for more. It is an incessant addiction that can never truly be satisfied.

- **Gluttony** is a failure to apply self-discipline, allowing compulsions to rule.

- **Envy** is the desire to have what others have. This is not limited to possessions; you can envy anything.

- **Sloth** is laziness, avoiding the opportunities life presents.

- **Wrath** is the desire to punish others for any perceived injustices. It is a reaction to the world not working as expected or believe it should. Intense anger is used as a form of retaliation and to control others to be submissive to our desires.

- **Pride and the narcissism of vanity** is the desire to be superior and revered. Pride, in this sense, is to refuse to acknowledge any personal flaws or mistakes. Narcissistic vanity is entwined with this pride—consumed with one's own appearance and self-importance.

The seven deadly sins are how you convince yourself to stay lost in compulsions and addicted to protecting the energy of your soul's unconsciousness. They cause you to forsake the purity of your soul's consciousness. Deliberately aligning with or succumbing to the seven deadly sins perpetuates your soul oppression, and you miss the mark of your original intention to resolve what inhibits your evolution.

Your soul oppression is the active force you generate from the energies stored in your soul's unconsciousness, which you use to emotionally, energetically, and physically oppress your awareness of your truth.

The energetic mass energy of mankind is the energetic structure of our collective unconsciousness, which is the unconsciousness of *True Source Divine Origin Consciousness*. It is the energetic storehouse for various types of soul-oppressive energy. This forms energetic collectives out of the reverberation of unresolved emotions and forms energetic barriers to truth out of mankind's control structures and belief systems. The energetic mass energy of mankind is the collective energy of every individual soul's unconsciousness—unresolved emotions.

True Source Divine Origin Consciousness

Your Soul's Consciousness

Heresy - Desire to control, indifference to truth, resentment of reality, oppositional energy, programming, conditioning and indoctrinations, guilt, shame, humiliation, denial of reality, disassociation from feeling

Controlled evolution - desire to control your soul denial with beliefs.

Images, illusions and controled identities.

Judgement, manipulation, confusion and control

Resistance, denial, avoidance and co-dependency.

Illusion
of control

Desire
to control

Soul Denial
Embedded Beliefs and Fears

Our individual soul's unconsciousness is the microcosm of unconsciousness.
It contributes to the energetic mass energy of mankind, which is the macrocosm of unconsciousness.

Being Mindful of Your Own Evolution

When you seek to participate in your own resolution and spiritual evolution,
allow yourself to be present in the exploration of yourself, truth, and life.
Be mindful of your core essences.

Take note of your contribution to life, repetitive cycles, and
acknowledge the futility of an image.

Be willing to explore all that is exposed to you without harsh self-judgement,
but with the grace required to comprehend, accept, and learn from your own reality.

Accept that spiritual evolution is a process and that you do not evolve overnight;
it can be so gradual that it is only on reflection you realise you have changed.

Be careful of being obsessed with analysing every morsel of your life with the desire
to determine what is of value and worth.
If you seek to comprehend the cause and effect of everything,
you will become self-obsessed and consumed with your desire for control.

Accept life as it unfolds.
Be present and honest about your own observations, reactions, and responses.

Trust that you will experience all you require to evolve.
Be aware of yourself within the reality of your interactions with life, others, and yourself.

Honour your awareness of truth.
It is your awareness that enables you to be insightful and introspective.
Evolution stems from self-reflection.

SECTION 1

Spirituality Is Nurturing Your Soul

Everyone has their own way of nurturing their soul or
feeling attuned with their authenticity.
Finding the experiences that enable you to do this
is part of the evolutionary journey.

For some it is meditation, praying as a group, playing music,
spending time in nature, playing golf,
or ....

Spirituality is whatever enables you to resonate the truth of yourself,
even if it is for a brief moment that reminds you of
an inner connection to the true essence
of who you are.

Nurturing Your Soul

CHAPTER ONE
Religion and Spirituality

Religion and spirituality shouldn't be confused, although for some they are entwined. How we perceive spirituality and religion will differ for each of us—as it should, because both are related to our souls.

How we relate to our own soul and the ways we choose to have a relationship with our origins is a personal choice, and we should respect that each of us has the right to choose.

We don't have the right to interfere with each other's freewill. To do so is a sign of lust for control and power. When others and organisations attempt to dictate how we should worship our origins, or believe they are entitled to control us to their expectations, under the guise that it will put us in good favour with the deity of their choice, they are worshipping power and control.

Our connection to our souls or our origins should not stem from a fear or be done under duress, because that is a dictatorship. Our religion or spiritual connection to our origins should nurture our journey of life, our relationship with each other, and our souls.

The following two pages include some common themes of differences between religion and spirituality. Don't forget it is important to have your own views. At the bottom of each page is an invitation to acknowledge what your personal views are.

Feet-on-the-ground spirituality entails understanding ourselves, including our point of view. Our opinions are changeable, and it's not about being right. It's about understanding why you feel a certain way. Each of us brings our life experiences to the expedition of ourselves, thus our opinions may vary. However, if we fundamentally respect the uniqueness of each soul and their journey, and cause no harm, our difference of opinions opens us to new avenues to explore and contemplate.

What Are Religions?

1. Religions are defined by their beliefs, rituals, and a set of rules laid out by those who have become an authority in their religion, often steeped in tradition.

2. Religions are organisations that offer a connection to their deity through the avenue they choose. There is a hierarchical system in place that clings to history and is generally reluctant to change, unless the change increases their power over people.

3. Being religious is having blind faith in the beliefs, rituals, and principles that they have either been indoctrinated into or they have chosen to adhere to by selecting the religion.

4. Some find an identity and a sense of belonging within their religious group, and this gives them comfort. It is an avenue they explore as they search for meaning in their existence.

5. Religious people want or believe their loyalty to their beliefs, rituals, and set of rules pleases what they consider to be their deity.

6. Religious people believe their religion is the true path to connecting with their deity and will help them grow spiritually. However, some become narrow-minded and oppositional to anything that doesn't sit in the realm of what they want to believe. This can also occur in those who claim to be spiritual but not religious.

7. Religions have been used throughout history as points of division and have sustained power struggles over what is the right belief, the more important deity, or who is entitled to have ownership over what others should believe is *the truth*.

8. Religion has been used to justify the oppression of those who do not fit into the ideals of the religion. Throughout history, they have created pecking orders of who is deemed as superior or inferior, often demonising those who do not conform to the rules and expectations of the religion.

9. Religion is aligning with beliefs and operating from beliefs.

10. Acknowledge what your personal views are: ………………………………….

What Is Spirituality?

1. Spirituality is exploring who you are and how you react to the adventure of life. It is acknowledging you are in a process—a journey to understand yourself and your relationship with your origins.

2. Spirituality is a personal pursuit that may take you to explore many beliefs and rituals so you can find what resonates with your soul. To resonate with your soul means to feel a conscious connection to truth and yourself at the same time. *Personal* doesn't mean solo, but it is taking responsibility for yourself and being accountable for the choices you make.

3. Spirituality is open-mindedness. It is working from an awareness of not having all the answers. It is questioning and challenging beliefs, observations, and exploring the meaningfulness of our existence, our interactions, and our relationships.

4. Spirituality is a recognition of being part of a bigger picture. Just like a grain of sand is part of the beach, each grain is different but significant to the health and wholeness of the beach. Spirituality is intentionally exploring the meaningfulness of who you are and accepting that we are all equal in significance, regardless of our position in life.

5. Spirituality is acknowledging you have a cause and effect on life and those you encounter. This means you strive to be of truth and respond respectfully to others and their unique path in life. It is seeking connection and equality, not power or control.

6. Spirituality is the willingness to be inspired by truth. This could be about yourself, feelings or the reality of an event. It is also about being of your authenticity. This may inspire others to be of their individual uniqueness. It is the journey of learning from your life experiences, being present and honest about your feelings, beliefs, and observations.

7. In recent history, spirituality has often been used to manipulate people into giving away their autonomy to someone who is exploiting their search for meaning and purpose. They often portray themselves as a conduit for the divine, offering spiritual elitism. This is also found under the guise of religion.

8. Spirituality is knowing we are all individually connected to divinity.

9. Spirituality is a process of understanding your uniqueness, independence, and individuality. It is the acceptance that our life journeys are different. Spirituality isn't buying into beliefs that portray the illusion that you can bypass the process of resolving what is unresolved within you.

10. Spirituality is seeking truth to be of truth.

11. Acknowledge what your personal views are:

    ....

    ....

CHAPTER TWO
Spirituality

S pirituality is not easy to sum up, because it's about the complexities of your relationship with yourself, truth, your origins, life, and others. Spirituality is asking meaningful questions and objectively observing our reactions to the journey required to find the answers. It's looking within, leaning into the unknown or the discomfort of discovering what we prefer to keep hidden in the shadow of denial. Spirituality is allowing ourselves to be part of revealing the truth that enables us to find answers for our internal curiosity.

By the way, objectively observing yourself is one of the hardest parts of spirituality. How do you objectively observe yourself while inundated with unresolved emotions, beliefs, and fears that taint your objectivity? *This is a question to ponder, many more to come.*

Spirituality is steeped in honest contemplation about matters that affect your awareness of your soul.

> ***One question leads to another.***
> ***One answer can open up a new direction to explore.***
> ***It is your curiosity that has you asking the questions,***
> ***committing to finding a truthful answer, and***
> ***opening the door to new directions.***
> ***Value your curiosity.***

Spirituality is the exploration of the:

- Meaning of life.

- Relevance of your origins.

- Uniqueness of who you are.

- Importance of your relationships with others.

- Unresolved emotions, beliefs, and fears you carry.

- Significance of discovering the truth of anything that once eluded you.

- Acknowledge what your personal views are ....

  ....

Spirituality is acknowledging the importance of:

- Discovering truth.

- The dynamically changing journey of life.

- The expansion of the consciousness of your origins.

- Taking an opportunity to participate in the processes that result in the expansion of your own soul's consciousness and evolution.

- The events derived from your relationships with others which create and expose you to crossroads—moments of choice—that initiate paths to explore and reveal truth to you.

- Acknowledge what your personal views are ....

....

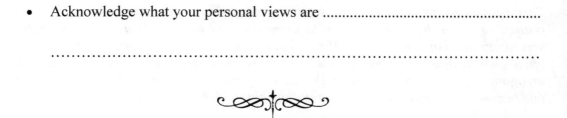

You are part of something bigger than your present comprehension. I think we can all accept that concept. Spirituality is an acceptance that life is a journey of exploration and search for meaning. It is an acceptance of being part of a process that enables you to discover the truth of your consciousness and to evolve into the purity of your soul. To do this, you must resolve what you have created and stored in your unconsciousness. Resolve the emotional baggage you carry.

Spirituality is exploring, learning, and expanding your understanding of yourself. Spirituality is connectedness to all that relates to your soul.

Your connection to your soul gives true value to your soul. It means the true value of your soul is recognised and acknowledged, which enables you to attune to the purposefulness of your existence. It also expands your awareness of the true value of your origins, the equality of all souls, and of yourself as the interface between consciousness and unconsciousness.

Being attuned to your consciousness is connectedness to the authenticity of your soul. It requires effort to reconnect with who you naturally are. However, every time you resolve something that separates you from being aware of yourself as a soul, it becomes more effortless to be of your authenticity. What is stored in your soul's unconsciousness is what you use to interrupt your awareness of your soul and causes you to withdraw from who you naturally are.

Function means the natural purpose. Evolution is the function of life, and you get to decide when and how you align with this purpose of life.

Hopefully you recognise the true value of this statement, *Spirituality is connectedness to all that relates to your soul*. It is your recognition and connection that gives it value. When you understand why you resonate with something—a statement, experience, feeling, or interaction with another—you acknowledge the true value of your insight and awareness. You awaken to the purpose of spirituality.

The way you value your spirituality will determine how mindful you are of the importance of being authentic and loyal to your soul. It is also recognising when you are off-kilter with the true essence of your soul. Knowing what is authentic and what is off-kilter requires you to be inquisitive and truthful; otherwise, you may fall into the trap of posturing spirituality, which impedes truthfulness and shuts down curiosity.

Posturing means to behave in a way that is intended to impress or mislead. Those who posture are also drawing attention to themselves, as they try to make people believe something that isn't true. It's artificial and stems from a non-genuine attitude. This is often seen in those who portray themselves as spiritually elite and operate from the arrogance of superiority. People with inflated spiritual egos have delusions of grandeur and become extremely toxic in their relationships with others.

Everyone on a spiritual journey will be confronted by their spiritual ego, and none of them are pretty. They sneak up on you and slowly build until you don't recognise your own arrogance. If you catch your ego at the stage of feeling a sense of superiority, it is wise to remind yourself of the equality of all souls and to respect the uniqueness of everyone's life journey and the importance of truthfulness. The secret is to not permit yourself to ignore your reality.

Feet-on-the-ground spirituality enables you to keep evolving while authentically experiencing the truth of your journey. However, if you have ignored the internal unrest within your soul, warning you of your spiritual ego and constructed beliefs that you use to shield yourself from your reality, you could become lost in an image of consciousness and an illusion of control. When you override the pangs of guilt for aligning with or fabricating lies that feed your ego, you support the false image.

You know your spiritual ego is running amok, when:

- You claim to be ascended, believing you exist beyond this earthly plane.

- You have become overly concerned with proving to others that you are spiritually elite and therefore deserve to be revered.

- You operate from the belief that you have resolved all your emotional issues, while denying your emotions and the truth of your behaviour.

- You suffer from the classic messiah complex that you were born to heal the world.

If you're using the belief that it's your mission in life to talk for the divine and to decide who else is specially chosen for a spiritual mission to justify all your behaviours that exploit, judge, or ignore the value of others, you are aligning with your spiritual ego and forsaking your soul.

The longer you align with your spiritual ego, the more narcissistic you'll become. If you find yourself treating others disrespectfully and being indifferent to the cause and effect of your behaviour, it is time to address the spiritual ego. This requires complete honesty. If you are unable to do so, you will eventually find the energy you generate with your ego, such as indifference and deception, becomes overwhelming. This affects you emotionally, mentally, and physically, and some form of breakdown will occur. The more you are able to tolerate your own indifference, arrogance, and ignorance, the longer you'll walk the path of narcissistic spiritual posturing.

Spirituality posturing is a trap that is easy to fall into, because it's about feeding your ego while disregarding your behaviour. It's about saying the words you believe convey a spiritual understanding, portraying an image of consciousness or the pretence of being an evolved soul. However, posturing impedes your opportunity to be *real*. True spirituality is expressing the authenticity of your soul. This means you have an understanding of yourself and are not creating an image—you are being present.

Being an evolving soul means you know you have a lot to learn and
are willing to be honest about the exploration of truth, yourself,
and the world you live in.

Spirituality does not come with rules, because you are unique. It is not an ideology or theology used to create performances; it is understanding your philosophy and values. Spirituality is acknowledging what resonates with your soul, valuing your own resonance with your awareness of truth and an acceptance of the equality of all souls. It also enables you to view the diversity of life experiences as unique opportunities to explore whatever is revealed.

Spirituality is about being present in the world you live in and conscious of yourself, your behaviour, and the words you speak. It stems from an awareness that you contribute energy to this world, and you choose what is of value to you.

Spirituality is an acknowledgment of the soul and an awareness that life is an exploration of all aspects of yourself.

We have created our unconsciousness—the storehouse of our emotional baggage—with the energy that does not naturally reside within our souls. Our unconsciousness has developed because we have not accepted, embraced, or understood the exquisiteness of who we are. Instead, we sought to have control over truth and each other. We, as mankind, have gotten lost in our image of ourselves, believing truth was something we could possess to supply power and control. Beliefs, instead of the pursuit to understand truth, became hidden agendas that have corrupted many religions and spiritual explorers.

Spirituality doesn't stem from beliefs or religion. It's knowing your authentic self and acknowledging you are on a journey to uncover the truth of your soul, resolving what is not of your true nature. Spirituality is not following a set of rules of what being conscious or evolved is portrayed as, it is being of your truth. Spirituality is not being submissive to another who wants you to believe they have a higher connection to our origins. It is embracing the journey of discovering your own connection to our origins—divinity and the divinity within your soul.

Spirituality is understanding your own value system and
having the integrity to trust what nurtures your soul.

Story of Awareness Overridden

I was talking to a young man at a spiritual fair who was struggling with the concept of consciousness. He had followed a guru and ended up disillusioned and confused about what being spiritual meant. He informed me he was now seeking guidance from a psychic because he felt she had answers for him, and he believed she worked from her higher consciousness.

I began to explain the virtues of understanding his own value system and questioned him on what he thought was important to him.

His reply was, "I don't know. I'm just in the sea of confusion. I even had to get away for a while and stayed in an isolated ski cabin because I feared I could go insane trying to be ..." He trailed off, unable to finish his sentence.

I explained spirituality wasn't the perfection of being Zen-like, nonreactive or impressing and appeasing everyone. It's about being real, being honest about what you are feeling and experiencing, recognising your unresolved emotions, and dealing with your suppressed wounds. Evolution is transformation through understanding, coming to terms with reality and respecting the uniqueness of who you are and your experience of life.

I told him, "Spirituality is not performing, and you seem to have fallen into the trap that if you get the performance right it means you are spiritual. You knew something wasn't right with the guru you followed, and you overrode your own awareness. Now you're struggling because what you wanted to be true has now been proven to be an illusion."

He nodded, and then explained, "The guru said I was special, and I so wanted to believe that he was right. I wanted to escape this internal feeling of inferiority and inner confusion."

I smiled and replied, "You are back where you started, but you are now aware of how important truthfulness and honesty are. I hope you spend some time reflecting on how aware you were of the dishonesty, and your insight into how posturing spirituality can be dangerous to your mental health."

It was as if the statement was a signal, because the next thing I knew, from out of nowhere, was his psychic lady wedging herself in between us. Her back and shoulders were blocking my view. Our conversation was cut short as she was announcing to the young man that his mother had told her she should introduce him to another female client, and it was time for him to be in a relationship.

I took a step back and smiled as the psychic turned to acknowledge that I was there. I watched as the young man struggled against her forcefulness, managing to say, "I'm not in the right frame of mind to be dating, as you know."

That seemed to ignite her willingness to go full speed ahead into unadulterated manipulation. "You know, your mother told me she feared you'd end up with a slant-eyes. Now listen to me. When I finish on stage, follow me, and I'll set up an introduction. Your mother thinks she is perfect for you. You don't want her disappointed, do you?" She had raised her hands to her eyes and slanted them mockingly before she dramatically turned and headed for the stage.

I could see the young man was embarrassed as he stood mumbling to the floor. I stood there, fascinated that he considered this psychic as working from a higher consciousness. With eyes wide open in disbelief, I asked, "When did your mother pass away?"

He replied, "Two months ago. I miss her deeply."

"I'm going to give you a tip: I don't believe your mother is racist, nor did she send a message to that psychic."

"She wasn't. I went to an Asian country after she died, but she knew it was a place I wanted to go to. She only ever wanted me to be happy." He replied.

I smiled and responded, "You obviously have told the psychic of your travels, who is now using that information to create a lie, she is attempting to sell to you. You have to work out if you are going to buy into this lie or work from what you know to be true."

He nodded and wandered off.

This was a moment that would show if he had learnt the importance of trusting his own awareness.

About an hour later, I saw him following the psychic.

All these experiences this young man is having are creating the building blocks that he requires to recognise what is unresolved within himself. This is part of his journey, and he will repeat what is unresolved until he is ready to deal with it. We can't always learn something straight away. We can hear truth, even recognise it for ourselves, but struggle to resist the compulsion to act out our unresolved emotions, beliefs, fears, wants, and desires.

Sometimes the realisations that create resolution take time to process before we put them into action. We have to recognise the value of our own awareness and be prepared to confront the truth of what we do and why we do it. Becoming honest with ourselves is not easy, especially when we do not understand the undercurrents of our unconsciousness.

It is easy for us as an outside observer to recognise the lesson. However, when we are in a whirlpool of conflicting emotions and suffer from excessive mind chatter that feeds our insecurities, it is difficult to acknowledge it. We all have our individual paths to walk.

Conscious Energy

Unconscious   Energy

OBSERVING THE ENTIRETY

Contemplation Exercise

S pirituality is an expedition of your awareness of yourself. Take a minute and contemplate the following points that spark your curiosity or annoyingly draw your attention. Contemplation is awareness building and a way of recognising what does or does not resonate with your soul. Allow yourself the time to explore what you value and the inner questions you have about spirituality.

Contemplate your thoughts about the statements. What stands out to you, and how does it make you feel?

We discount our feelings easily. However, the more attuned to them we are, the more honest we are about ourselves. Within a spiritual journey, we are challenging and often debunking our own beliefs. This can be difficult until we realise, they are barriers to a true soul exploration. Recognising any misconceptions and knowing what we value is part of the journey.

It's easy to fool ourselves, especially when we want to. The more aware we are of ourselves the less we want to be fooled.

If you are a journaler, write down your thoughts, insights, and feelings. Come back at a later date and, without looking at what you previously wrote, do the same statement, then compare. What changed? What is the same? Write down your conclusion about the comparison. Do this as many times as you like with varying degrees of time in between.

Add your own statement to point 7..................................... that you believe is important to you. After all, this is your exploration.

Spirituality Is

1. Spirituality is to be aware of yourself as an evolving soul, willing to learn from your life experiences, relationships with others, and your resonance with truth. *It is not using the language associated with truth manipulatively or for the purpose of creating an image, or to sustain an illusion.*

2. Spirituality is endeavouring to uncover the meaningfulness of your existence and experiences. *It is not bypassing the truth.*

3. Spirituality is trusting your resonance with truth and valuing your internal knowing. *It is not arrogantly portraying yourself as elite or using spirituality as a position of power over others.*

4. Spirituality is recognising what nurtures your relationship with yourself. *It is not ignoring the reality of yourself and the way you treat others.*

5. Spirituality is personal growth that is in tune with the essence of your soul. *It is not ego driven.*

6. Spirituality is embracing the responsibility of freedom. *It is not abdicating responsibility.*

7. Spirituality is ....

....

....

....

Spirituality Is Not

1. Spirituality is not beliefs. *It is resonating with an internal knowing.*

2. Spirituality is not imitating another or performing an image. *It is expressing the truth of your soul.*

3. Spirituality is not about following the rules another has set out for you. *It is the freedom to be yourself while respecting the equality of all souls.*

4. Spirituality is not a belief system that organises the way you think or tells you what is important. *It is discovering the importance of your integrity and knowing what you value.*

5. Spirituality is not about disrespecting or harming others because they think or align with different beliefs. *It is accepting the diversity of life experiences and respectfully acknowledging that it is our differences that expose the unique opportunities we can experience on earth.*

6. Spirituality is not for the purpose of judging yourself superior or inferior to others or a method of expanding your ego. *It is recognising your opportunity to connect truthfully with yourself, life, and others. It is for the purpose of recognising, expressing, and being of truth.*

8. Spirituality is not ....

....

....

....

SECTION 2

*Evolution is the process of liberating yourself
from the ways in which you oppress the truth of your soul.*

CHAPTER THREE
Judgement Impedes Spiritual Evolution

Our judgement is one of our greatest hurdles to overcome. Judgement creates many pitfalls that impede spiritual growth. Our judgement of what constitutes spiritual evolution causes us to become lost, chasing an illusion.

There is a popular illusion that we should have an enlightened moment or major event in which everything falls into place, and we will operate from that moment forth at a higher frequency. It is true we can have enlightened moments and events where we converge on internal knowledge that puts something in perspective. These moments are pieces of our life's jigsaw, but they are never the entire picture. Evolution develops from multiple moments, and each moment should be celebrated and the learning embraced. We would be fools to believe evolution occurs in a moment. Even when we have profound enlightened moments that cause a major shift, there will be a period in the aftermath of comprehending the shift.

Our judgement of how spiritual evolution should occur can leave us devaluing everyday life. This can cause us to seek places, people and situations we believe will be more conducive to an enlightened moment. This leaves us trying to orchestrate spiritual moments or creating filters of self-manipulation that we use to convince ourselves of what we want to believe. Unfortunately, we often miss the moments we can learn from because we are too busy trying to create one.

Unlikely Moment of Clarity Story

This was a moment that heightened my awareness, as it made me look at judgement differently—a moment of clarity. There was no spiritual background music, mood lighting, fragrant candle or spiritual guru sharing his wisdom. No, for twenty-four-year-old me—that's a while ago—it was in a rowdy pub, busting to go to the loo, heading for it at the speed of knots, when a falling-off-his-chair drunk grabbed my arm, pulled me towards him, and in a slurring voice announced, "Look at them, Lorraine. They are all worried about what others think of them! They should be worrying about how they feel about themselves and be someone they like instead of wanting others to tell them if they are good enough." This hit me like a brick, as it is so true and makes so much sense.

Everyone is worried about what others think of them. They don't really acknowledge the truth of themselves. They are stuck in the fear of judgment and use judgement to define themselves. Judgement is at the forefront, instead of self-acceptance or the acceptance of life being a tapestry of differences.

Why worry about what others think? I'm the one who has to live with myself and look at myself in the mirror. I'm the one who chooses how I treat others and myself. The sage drunk's words ignited a thousand questions, and I realised how fascinating we are and how lost we are.

As I returned from the toilet, I went back to the sage drunk, quietly saved him from falling off his chair, propped him up, and said, "I get what you're saying."

His reply was, "What, love? What do you get?"

I explained what his previous statement made me think about. His response was, "Bloody hell, girl, getting a bit deep. You better get another drink. I'm not sure what you're on about!"

Got to love that—moment of clarity gone for him, but I still remember it.

Spiritual moments are often not orchestrated by us. Spiritual moments are moments of realisation, and it takes many for us to comprehend ourselves. Believing that evolution occurs in one huge, powerful moment, instead of recognising the increments of growing awareness through our numerous life events, impedes our spiritual growth. We can chase experiences we believe will validate our beliefs and desires instead of being present in what we are experiencing. The desire for an enlightened experience can leave us negatively judging ourselves when we expect our lives to drastically change after a moment of realisation, but they don't.

Realisations are stepping-stones that head us toward spiritual evolution, build our awareness, and contribute to our soul maturity.

When we become reliant on our judgement to determine what is valuable, we become embroiled in the duality of judgement. This can leave us wanting to know what is right or wrong, conscious or unconscious, good or bad. The desire to know can become torturous, and instead of being present and honest about what we feel, observe, and are motivated by, we anchor to the desire to secure being right in our own judgement.

Wanting to be right and in command of truth is a spiritual pitfall that impedes soul maturity. It sets up the chase to prove that what we believe is right. This leaves no room for exploration and allows our judgement to become a worshipped weapon. A weapon against searching for truth, for what resonates with our souls and investigating the cause and effect of our judgement. When we no longer challenge our judgement, it morphs into perceived righteousness.

When we are consumed by the energy of our unconsciousness, we operate from wants and desires, one of which is the desire to protect our own judgement. This desire becomes a distorted instinct—a compulsion. We are blinded by our desire to be right. We assume being right is a reflection of our superiority, which gives us a surge of control energy. Interestingly, we also surge with control energy when we get away with deception, are able to manipulate another to get what we want, or scoffing at others while believing we are superior to them.

Inherent and compulsive reactions or actions are done without conscious thought; it is allowing ourselves to act impulsively or from an unresisted urge often with the lack of awareness as to why we feel compelled. Evolution requires thought, awareness, understanding, and retained knowledge.

> *Knowing what motivates our instincts,*
> *compulsions, and disposition is a*
> *precursor to evolution.*

We are the interface of both our consciousness and unconsciousness, and we can instinctively or reactively operate from either. The pivotal point is the decision of what we value, and we are constantly experiencing the freedom to choose, question, and challenge our unconscious instincts.

Knowing what is motivating our instincts enables us to understand what part of our system we have aligned with. When we align with the energy of our unconsciousness, there is often an internal flash of concern, that reveals an awareness of not resonating with the truth of who we are. In a split second, we have to choose to either acknowledge the awareness or to deny it. When we elect to deny it, we use our judgement to justify what we're doing, and then we treat our judgement as if it were a truth. This creates perceived righteousness, which means we have morphed the judgement into something we no longer want to question or challenge. So, we constantly reinforce the judgement. Lies become acceptable, and indifference to truth becomes tolerable.

> *Judgement is fickle.*
> *Our intent and desires fuel*
> *the judgement and determine*
> *what will be judged and how it will be judged.*

Life exposes us all to countless experiences. We have to patiently remain present as life unfolds to truly comprehend the reality of what has occurred or is occurring. When we operate from the duality of judgement, we can become indecisive and unable to comprehend our own reality. We see-saw from one conflicting opinion, want, or belief to another, and each is fuelling the indecision. We often find ourselves believing something is good because it suits our agenda. Then, in the next minute, we decide it's bad because it's inconvenient to another agenda. As we align with different agendas our desires and intent change, making it difficult to decide what to do or what to accept as truth. This inhibits our ability to seek truth and instead we seek to validate our judgement. Our see-sawing generally exposes something we wish to ignore.

Operating from the duality of judgement causes us to become contrary to our integrity. This can leave us seeking only what we believe is of value to the image we want to portray. We can also become fixated on upholding illusions, or securing our beliefs. This inhibits our willingness and ability to be truthfully honest with ourselves, which impedes our spiritual evolution.

Our judgement and beliefs entwine, and become influencers that corrupt many of our good intentions. We become reluctant to acknowledge the reality of our judgement and beliefs, and yet silently use them as motivation. One such entwined belief and judgement is the expectation that spirituality should be rewarded. We expect our wants and desires to be appeased and can judge ourselves as inferior if they are not. We can easily fall into the trap of believing our wants and desires entitle us to a sense of superiority, especially if they are appeased. We can fool ourselves that our judgement is as good as truth. This sets us on a path to prove we are superior to others, which becomes the agenda we adhere to, and leaves us in competition with others. Our judgement replaces our awareness of truth, which corrupts our relationship with our soul. This means honesty becomes a commodity that we trade for results and control.

Your soul and honesty are not commodities.
Your honesty reflects your willingness to care for and nurture your soul.

When you trade your honesty to protect an image of yourself, you lose a sense of self and your integrity. It is easy to become lost in your denial of reality and seduced by your own image, but these separate you from the authenticity of your soul.

When you separate from valuing your soul, evolution and awakened consciousness become concepts you arrogantly play with. You can use them as a guise to conceal the reality of your desire to control or even as an avenue to act out your indifference to truth. These are choices you make. When you become willing to explore the motives behind your choices and acknowledge your intent, you are choosing to be truthful.

Spiritual evolution is the process of living, learning
and comprehending the truth of yourself.

When we truly look at our judgement,
it is not that hard to hurdle over, and it opens up a new path to explore.
But if we refuse to acknowledge what is stopping us
from examining the truth of our judgement, we will never move.

Suppressed but Impacting Story

Years ago, I had an interesting session with a woman I knew as a child. She was running meditation classes, and she prided herself on her spiritual wisdom. It was a fascinating experience. Towards the end of the session, I tapped into her resentment for not being, in her opinion, "rewarded properly" for her spirituality. She was reluctant to talk about it when I first questioned her, so I explained how dealing with the resentment might make her feel better about herself.

Even when something is hidden and not spoken about, it is still having an impact. It can be surprising how the energy is influencing our reactions to our life experiences.

When people become consumed with their spiritual image they are reluctant to address the energy of their soul's unconsciousness—their stored emotional baggage. They prefer to believe they no longer have any unresolved emotions and have accepted their past; therefore, they have evolved beyond having to concern themselves. Some will acknowledge these emotions and override their awareness with layers of spiritual concepts until they have convinced themselves the emotions have passed.

Spirituality is an acknowledgement of our truth, knowing there is a process of evolution if we are prepared to be honest about what is impeding the flow of our consciousness.

Reluctantly, she began to explain what she resented. She had divorced many years ago and never returned to the same financial circumstances. She was still single and no longer a property owner. She announced with conviction that she had been patient, zealously followed her regimen of saying affirmations, and gave freely of herself to others in matters of spiritual encouragement and soothing their emotional angst. This ended with the proclamation, "When is it my turn?"

I asked, "What rewards were you expecting, and how should they arrive?"

She replied enthusiastically as she began to entwine her judgement of her deservedness and belief of entitlement into the momentary plan of speaking honestly about the missing piece to getting what she believed she was owed.

"I want a house of my own, a spiritual man who knows and respects my wisdom, and gives me financial security. Is that too much to ask for? I could win the lottery or be gifted. I don't care how it arrives. I just want it to happen!"

I asked, "What if it doesn't?"

"It has to! I say my affirmations!" She replied.

I asked, "In your belief, does it matter what energy and intention is fuelling your affirmations?"

She replied her energy was sound and started to recount the beginning of our session and how she was impressed with what had come up for her.

I asked if she knew she was deflecting and was shutting down an issue she should address. I said, "Maybe today is not the day, but think about it."

I gave her some concepts to consider about resentment in general. She nodded and smiled.

She then explained she had an experience with me, when I was a child. She explained I had asked her about something no one knew and had freaked her out. I had apparently asked her if her new boyfriend would upset her husband and if she was scared she was going to hurt her husband.

We laughed about how freaky that would have been, and she said she had often wondered if I had remembered it. I didn't know she had an affair. Actually, I was surprised by it. I presume I read the energy and must have said what I read. I have no memory of this event, but I didn't doubt what she was saying. I could feel her sincerity.

She ended the affair after this and resented not being able to be with her lover, although he wasn't interested in a permanent relationship. It was just a lovers' tryst when he came to town four or five times a year. I reiterated to her that I had no memory of the conversation.

We reminisced about different things, which I found interesting, as she had an adult's point of view, and I had a child's memory. We were laughing and giggling and hugged goodbye. As she placed her hand on the doorknob—ready to return to her world and as I was back sitting at the desk, she turned towards me with steely eyes and said, "What if I leave here and tell everyone you are full of shit? Nothing you'd said made any sense— just babble?"

I was taken aback by this, took a minute to catch up to what was now occurring, and replied, "Both you and I know what happened in your session. You can choose to be dishonest, and I have no control over what you do or say."

She stared at me, pondering the next statement.

I smiled and said, "Resentment is hard to contain, isn't it?"

Spirituality is not a performance we switch on and off. What is suppressed bubbles to the surface so we can discover what is burdening our soul. In these moments, we reveal our underbelly—our unconsciousness. This is an opportunity to address our unresolved emotions, fears, and embedded beliefs. We often run because we fear our underbelly defines who we are. However, it defines only what requires resolving so we can be unified with the truth of our souls. It also defines what's filling the space of our separation from our awareness of our truth.

Resolve the separation from the truth of your soul and you will evolve.

Spiritual evolution requires us to be truthfully honest about ourselves and to examine what is influencing us. It involves acknowledging our actions, patterned behaviours, the words we speak, and our intent. It requires us to challenge our beliefs, to explore the motives of our judgement, and to examine the cause and effect of the unresolved emotions.

Our experiences with each other are an arena to learn from. We are souls, and our paths cross to expose each other to the truth of what is stored within that is impeding our spiritual growth. We have the freedom to decide if we are willing to be truthful about ourselves or to orchestrate denial of reality. We learn from what occurs, how we react, and from what we trigger in each other. Sometimes it is not pleasant; at other times it is a beautiful moment of clarity. When we are willing to be truthful with ourselves, our shared life experiences are very revealing.

We can attempt to use beliefs to overshadow the reality of our unconscious energy and judgement to alter our awareness. However, it is our unconscious energy that holds us back from the true potential of our souls. When we're willing to acknowledge what impedes spiritual growth and what nurtures it, we are able to be more truthful about the moments that are convergent points, providing opportunities to build our understanding of ourselves.

Spiritual evolution is the result of expanding self-awareness.

CHAPTER FOUR
Spiritual Evolution Is Derived from Exploration

When we acknowledge it's a choice to participate in our spiritual evolution, we realise every soul is unique. We also realise another's soul journey is exposing truth to them, as our soul journey is exposing truth to us.

The word *derive* comes from the Latin word *derivare* which means "to lead from or draw off, such as a stream of water from its source". A stream can be traced back to its main source. It also means to descend from and flow.

> *You are the stream, life is the flow, and your source is divinity.*
> *You are part of a bigger system, one you may not fully understand,*
> *but know that is majestically significant to your existence.*
>
> **Divinity is the collective energy of your origins—**
> ***True Source Divine Origin Consciousness.***

Our spiritual evolution stems from uniting with the main source of our existence; it's moving and flowing with truth. It requires us to trace our stream back to its source, finding what is diverting our attention, polluting our water, damming our awareness, and creating whirlpools that cause us to become stuck. It requires us to acknowledge what is causing us to resist, deny, and avoid the truth of being a stream that is part of the river of life and the sea of truth.

Evolving souls are explorers keen to discover the reality of the stream and the connection to its water source. This means they will follow the stream, exploring all aspects of it, as they experience their expedition of self-discovery.

There are many steps and adventures that allow discovery and unification to occur. Each step is derived from a bigger journey, and each of us explore our own stream. Every expedition is unique.

Spiritual evolution is derived from exploration, and it requires us to choose to:

1. Be present in the reality of our life experience, acknowledging the truth of our behaviour and the cause and effect of our actions.

   Be aware of yourself and what you're doing. Acknowledge the energy associated with your words and actions and be mindful of their impact on others.

2. Examine what fuels our difficulty to take responsibility for the way we engage with ourselves, each other, life, and truth.

   Take responsibility for your own soul and for how your energy contributes to your experiences. Be accountable for how you treat others. Acknowledge your own awareness of truth.

3. Learn from our internal world.

   Acknowledge and accept the reality of both your soul's consciousness and unconsciousness. Accept that you are part of the process to free yourself from what oppresses your own unconditional love for yourself, others, and the truth.

4. Allow ourselves to be truthfully honest within our own exploration of the opportunities life, relationships, and truth presents.

   Life and all it entails exposes you to the truth of your energy, and you have the freedom to acknowledge or deny what is revealed.

5. Acknowledge the truth we are aware of without hiding our own soul insight.

   If you keep telling yourself what spiritual evolution has to be, you cannot honestly explore the uniqueness of your experience of yourself. You may become trapped attempting to orchestrate a performance you believe will prove to others that you are evolved. This will cause you to become lost in your own denial of reality, trapped by the images and illusions you cling to.

6. Be self-reflective and willing to take responsibility for the eternalness of your soul.

   Take accountability for your contribution to life and accept that you yearn to be of the purity of your soul, while having freewill. Give yourself the time to reflect your past and contemplate what you are aware of. This enables you to learn from life.

7. Acknowledge—we are—the opportunity for our consciousness to flow freely.

   Value your own consciousness and the core essences of your soul. Trust yourself to express your authenticity and support yourself within the vulnerability of revealing your truth.

8. Develop our awareness of truth.

   Develop an awareness of how truth feels to you. Be honest about tolerating your indifference to truth and value your integrity.

9. Spiritual evolution is derived from your

   ....

   ....

We potentiate our evolution when we accept the value of our awareness of our consciousness and acknowledge the opportunity to resolve the energy of our unconsciousness.

When we accept, we are an interface between our consciousness and unconsciousness, we realise the value of our truthfulness. Truthfulness becomes important when we trust we will be exposed to what needs to be resolved throughout and in conjunction with our life.

Acknowledgement Is Opportunity

Stepping-stones help us head in a direction and travel into the unknown. They help us navigate places where we are frightened or reluctant to land, because we fear it will inconvenience us, cause harm, or leave us in a situation we can't control. They can also be an action or an event that creates forward movement towards a goal or new awareness. We choose what we acknowledge, and we also choose whether the acknowledgement is going to be a stepping-stone to further exploration.

Acknowledgement of ourselves and what we are internally and externally experiencing, enables us to explore life. The exploration of life and ourselves creates growth in our awareness of truth, which leads to a greater understanding of our significance to truth. Evolution is unifying with the significance of truth.

> *Acknowledgement is a stepping-stone to exploration.*
> *Exploration builds awareness and understanding,*
> *and this is the precursor to spiritual evolution.*

Acknowledgement is the decision to accept the truth or the existence of something. It is the acceptance that allows us to move forward and grow spiritually. We can unconsciously or knowingly avoid recognising what will open the door to exploration. Especially, if we don't understand:

- What we fear.

- The beliefs we want to protect.

- How we worship the illusion of control.

- The compulsive desire to control.

Think of it as crossing a muddy stream—*the stream of beliefs, fears, and control structures*. We are aware of the stepping-stones—*having to be truthful to get to the other side*. We decide if we will walk that way or retreat. This is the same for acknowledgment—we decide whether to accept or deny. First, we have to address any fears, beliefs, and control structures that could obstruct our path to recognising truth, or we will use them to compulsively run away or slowly retreat while denying we are retreating.

Crossing the stream requires us to acknowledge what we are crossing. Sometimes it is a comfortable walk of discovery through observation and truthfulness. Other times we slip and fall into the mud, wallowing around for a while until we are prepared to get honest about what we are experiencing.

Before you truly acknowledge something, you automatically go into a decision-making process. The key is recognising you are making a decision.

We automatically assess the value of crossing the muddy stream—*the value of acknowledgement*. We question what is valuable to us. The more we understand our decision-making process, the more informed choices we make. Our choices are informed when we acknowledge the truth of ourselves and reality.

What motivates us to make the decisions we make reveals a lot to us. How we question ourselves may unmask some hidden beliefs, fears, and control structures that impede our spiritual evolution. As we acknowledge the truth of our reactions and responses, we begin to recognise opportunities to get real with ourselves.

We decide what we chose to acknowledge and any acknowledgement of truth—the truth of ourselves, others, or reality—enables us to keep exploring more truths. Exploration is exploring the unfamiliar, so we have to be prepared to deal with uncertainty and trust in the value of truth to keep going.

Exploration is the willingness to discover and thoroughly examine what we stumble across. It is recognising that there are layers to building an understanding. We might not see or comprehend everything at once. It is through our truthfulness that other layers appear. Exploration requires us to carefully consider what we become aware of.

Awareness is a knowing, an acceptance that stems from noticing and then being truthful about what you have noticed.

Stepping-Stone Exercise

Imagine you are standing beside a loved one who is thinking about using the stepping-stones to cross a muddy stream, and you can hear their thoughts.

You can hear the questions or statements they are prepared to acknowledge and the ones they would struggle to acknowledge or say out loud.

You will also be aware of what is motivating their questions and statements, such as fear, beliefs, or control structures.

How would you advise them?

- Stepping-stones represent being truthful on the journey to discover the truth of both their consciousness and unconsciousness. It is a journey that could be confronting.

- The muddy stream represents their energy. Instead of the water pristinely flowing from their origins, it is mixed and heavily burdened with the energy of their soul's unconsciousness: unresolved emotions, fears, embedded belief, control structures, barriers to truth, framework of soul oppression, and the seven deadly sins.

- The other side of the crossing represents unification with truth and growth in their understanding of themselves.

Listen to their thoughts—their internal questioning.

Acknowledge and have empathy for what is motivating them.

Then answer the questions and advise them.

1. Am I sure I want to get to the other side? Am I willing to accept this is a journey of discovery, or should I stay here? Why bother? This is motivated by fear.

    a)   What do you believe they fear?

        ....

        ....

    b)   How will they convince themselves to not bother?

        ....

        ....

    c)   Your advice is

        ....

        ....

2. I don't know what could happen during the crossing or what is on the other side. I need to know before I make a move. Shouldn't I know what to expect before I explore, so I can tell myself what to look for? This is motivated by control structures and beliefs.

    a)   What do you believe they want to control?

        ....

        ....

    b)   Why is building expectations so important to them?

        ....

        ....

    c)   Your advice is

        ....

        ....

3. I already know what all this is about, so I don't need to walk on the stepping-stones! I have completed this journey before. I don't need to do it again. I was born with this understanding and have had my enlighten experiences, so I don't need to bother with the exploration, as I already know! This is motivated by beliefs.

    a)   What are they exposing with this attitude?

        ....

        ....

    b)   What do you believe they fear losing?

        ....

        ....

    c)   Your advice is

        ....

        ....

4. I should find out first what the reward or prize is before I make the crossing. Do I want to acknowledge reality? Is it worth the effort? Am I prepared to accept what I find, or should I have an agenda, so I can override anything that doesn't suit me? This is motivated by control structures.

    a) What do you believe they want as a reward or prize?

        ....

        ....

    b) Why do you think they need an agenda?

        ....

        ....

    c) How are they interacting with reality?

        ....

        ....

    d) Your advice is

        ....

        ....

5. This is just a detour from my familiar route that I plan to return to! I only want to accept the parts that are desirable to me. I don't want to acknowledge anything undesirable. If it gets too much, can I reset to what is familiar and pretend I never attempted to cross? This is motivated by fear.

    a) How will they evaluate what is desirable or undesirable?

        ....

        ....

    b) Why is the familiar so important to them?

        ....

        ....

c) Your advice is

....

....

6. *Is exploring and acknowledging what I find going to get in the way of what I want? I already have plans. Does admitting the truth found in an exploration hinder or help me get what I want?* This is motivated by control structure.

a) What are their priorities?

....

....

b) What do you believe happens to most plans?

....

....

c) Your advice is

....

....

7. *Is acknowledging the truth going to inconvenience me? What could I lose, or are there any difficulties I will have to face because I have acknowledged a truth?* This is motivated by fear and control structures.

a) What do you believe will be their greatest difficulty?

....

....

b) How are they judging the value of truth?

....

....

c) Your advice is

....

....

8. *Will I be unscathed from the crossing? How does the exploration of myself affect my perception? Can I deny what I've learnt later if it causes me pain, trouble, or exposes too much for my liking? Will I be able to deny my awareness?* This is motivated by fear and control structures.

a) What do you think they fear?

....

....

b) What do you think they want to control?

....

....

c) Your advice is

....

....

9. *What if I slip and get muddy feet as I attempt to cross? What if this affects what I want to believe or makes me have to deal with issues I want to avoid? Could this cause me grief, and how will it affect me?* This is motivated by the protection of beliefs, fears, and control structures.

a) What do you think they fear slipping into?

....

....

b) What do you think will cause them the greatest grief?

....

....

c) Your advice is

....

....

10. What if I get over there to a new awareness and don't like what I can see? What if I don't like the idea of having to be responsible for what I know? What will change if I acknowledge what the crossing exposes to me? This is motivated by fear.

a) Why do they fear responsibility for their new awareness or internal knowing?

....

....

b) How does this attitude impede their awareness?

....

....

c) Your advice is

....

....

We give away our best advice, and often allow our own thoughts and
internal debates to hold us back.

Take notice of your advice and recognise the significance of
your awareness and insight.

*It is easier to see in others what you refuse to acknowledge within yourself.
Take the advice you would give your loved ones.*

Chapter Five
Life Is an Opportunity for Spiritual Evolution

L ife has a constant flow. Regardless of our planning, it is an event that takes us to experiences that expose the energy of both our soul's consciousness and unconsciousness. Life is like ageing; we may not like all factors of the process but some events are inevitable and unavoidable.

Spiritual evolution is a journey of discovery that continues throughout this life experience and beyond.

You exist; therefore, you are a traveller in your own life. How you react and respond to life contributes to your experience. You have freewill and can choose to remain a prisoner on your own merry-go-round of soul oppression, refusing to acknowledge the intricacies of the labyrinths of your life; or you can choose to explore these as life unfolds, realising there are many discoveries you can make from within the labyrinth.

Life is an unfolding experience—a labyrinth of events, relationships, and energetic experiences.

Life consists of moments of time joined together. That instance in time we just had is gone, but we can learn from it. We don't get to experience that exact instant again; it has passed. Life forces us to move forward. We can't fight time. It occurs, and we have no control over it. Each second is heading to the next, and we are on the ride that time provides.

Life creates changes in us, and our aging exposes us to this truth. However, change and evolution are not the same. Change of circumstances and in time doesn't equate to spiritual evolution. Regardless of the change, we can continue reacting and responding in the same manner. Spiritual evolution changes how we react or respond, leading to the development of our soul maturity.

Spiritual evolution is adapting to what is understood. It is important to retain and utilise what we have learnt. We can learn something, but if we do not utilise what we learn, it doesn't produce evolution. We can experience a moment of clarity and then override our understanding with whatever evokes a sense of familiarity, thus abandoning our new understanding. This will not create evolution, although there may be a change in our awareness.

You are always the pivotal point in how you experience life.

Evolution is transformation that occurs as a result of our adaptations from what we have understood, retained, and utilised. Evolution develops from action, putting what we understand into practice. It's our new awareness that assists us to unify with the truth within and to develop a broader understanding of ourselves.

You can have a concept of the conscious energy within your soul. However, if you do not utilise that energy, you are not evolving. You are just conceptualising something you are aware of, have heard about, or have intellectually studied.

> *Spiritual evolution is to be of your conscious energy,*
> *to be unified with it and to instinctually react and*
> *respond to life as a source of consciousness.*

For example, knowing there is kindness within you and choosing not to utilise it, causes you to oppose your spiritual evolution. When you are unwilling to unify with the core essences of your soul, you empower an unconscious energy to take its place. You don't realise you are doing this and it is how spiritual evolution is opposed. We have all experienced a moment of clarity and comprehended 'something', only to reject it later. Paradoxically, sometimes the process of comprehending something and then rejecting it, eventually destroys our ability to deny our awareness, which turns into true understanding. We often reject our awareness and refuse to unify with our core essences, when we fear losing control of something.

We have a tendency to reject our awareness and it isn't until we recognise the consequences that we understand the true value of our awareness.

Rejecting Awareness Story

Sally was emotionally troubled and easily sunk into bouts of depression. So, Lisa—her life-long friend, would phone to check on her and listened to her for hours. Lisa had supported Sally for years, through unemployment, divorce, family issues, and the ramifications of low self-esteem. Lisa helped with house chores when Sally's home descended into disarray. She organised social outings and made sure Sally felt loved and valued.

Sally was very appreciative of Lisa's kindness. She marvelled at how selfless and generous Lisa was. Lisa supported all her personal growth endeavours, on occasions drove her to support groups, paid for weekend retreats as birthday presents, and attentively listened to the new beliefs Sally was acquiring.

After a while, Sally's confidence returned. Life moved in a positive direction on many fronts. A new romantic partner entered her life, she was gainfully employed, and experiencing exciting travel adventures. Sally believed she had evolved and felt spiritually enriched. It warmed Lisa's heart to see Sally so happy. However, as life kept improving, Sally began to exploit Lisa as the babysitter, and would demand her to do house chores while visiting. She no-longer returned missed calls and only rang with demands.

Lisa tired of Sally's behaviour and started to distance herself. She became unavailable to babysit, was no-longer visiting, and only called on special occasions—birthdays and Christmas. She always answered Sally's calls, but politely excused herself, citing that she was presently busy.

Sally was disgruntled by Lisa's unwillingness to be at her beck and call. So, she ragefully rang and accused her of being a bad friend, betraying her, and treating her as if she was nothing.

Lisa replied, "I wish you well. Friendship to me, is not a duty or a job. I consider myself a good friend, I care, but refuse to be dictated to by someone who does not value me."

Sally was outraged, "Never call me, or my children again. I want nothing to do with you!"

Months passed, and eventually Sally realised that she had rejected her awareness of who Lisa was and how good she had been to her when she was troubled. She missed talking to a friend who truly cared about her. She realised as her life improved, that she had not been a good friend to Lisa. She had betrayed her kindness and treated her badly.

Sally knew the value of kindness and friendship, but had chosen to deny her awareness. She knew her friend had kept her sane during her darkest days and she had in return rejected valuing the friendship. When she felt back in control of her life, she took advantage of Lisa. She had become self-absorbed, turning the freely offered friendship into a dictatorship she controlled.

Sally realised she had exploited Lisa as a servant, and understood why she had distanced herself. She became angry at herself, for not valuing the friendship. Her rejection of her own awareness of the importance of kindness, meant she hadn't unified with her own core essences. She didn't operate from kindness, care, loyalty or love, all of which she once comprehended to be so valuable. She had operated from control, entitlement and indifference.

Sally knew kindness was important and chose not to utilise it herself. She comprehended the value of the friendship and of Lisa's kindness, and then rejected it. Paradoxically, this experience eventually destroyed her ability to deny her awareness of herself, which creates an opportunity to truly understand what is of value to her.

Sally feared losing control over her new life experiences and rejected her awareness, glossing over the reality of her behaviour, and devaluing her own and Lisa's core essences—kindness, care, loyalty and love.

We learn from our experiences. When we understand the true consequences of what we reject, this often leaves us bewildered by our own behaviour. We evolve as we use our understanding of truth, to influence our actions. Spiritual evolution is unification within ourselves, while unifying with truth.

When you oppose what you've understood
you create stagnation, impede spiritual growth,
and protect the immaturity of your soul.

Life provides opportunities to learn and to utilise what we've learnt. Any labyrinth you learn from, you will experience again, allowing you to practice what you've learnt. This will determine if you have evolved or if you are still developing. You may walk the same life experiences—the labyrinth, many times and each time learn new increments of truth. This builds your understanding. Once it is retained and utilised, it ignites evolution within your soul. This process is the journey of life.

Life is a labyrinth of discovery, and
one labyrinth can lead to another.
This is the journey of life.

Spiritual Evolution Is a Process

Spiritual evolution is a process that enables us to return freely to our natural state. Evolution occurs as we embrace and emanate the frequency of our soul's consciousness. This can be only experienced, not contrived.

Evolution occurs when we mindfully journey through life, experiencing the labyrinths we constructed from our own emotions, beliefs, fears, and control structures. This journey exposes us to the energy of our soul's unconsciousness. Labyrinths also show us how we use what is stored and carried in our soul's unconsciousness to overshadow the core essences of our soul.

Spiritual evolution requires us to enter the pathways and passages we created from the complicated, convoluted, and intricate webs of misleading perceptions about ourselves and reality. We are the creators of our unconsciousness, but we are also our own liberators.

The process of evolution occurs through resolution. It is a process of discovering the truth of our own creation and resolving the energy that does not naturally resonate with or emanate from our soul. As we engage with and process our way through our life experiences, realising the value of our truthfulness, we begin to embrace life's opportunities.

Evolution is experiencing the autonomy of your being,
while cherishing life as a shared experience that our presence contributes to.

When we operate from and project the energy of our unconsciousness, we contribute unconscious energy to life and our relationships with others and ourselves. When we refuse to be truthful and can no longer justify our own energy displayed in our behaviour, revealed in the words we speak and use as motivation for the way we judge everyone and everything, we begin to fortify our merry-go-round of soul oppression. This leaves us stagnant until we acknowledge the truth of ourselves. *If you feel like you are on a treadmill, you are aware of your stagnation.*

This type of stagnation causes us to withdraw from respecting our own soul's consciousness, reality, and objectivity, which leads to embodying and protecting the energy within our soul's unconsciousness. This creates various forms of indifference to truth. We become trapped on the merry-go-round of soul oppression, rejecting our own truth, and operating from indifference. This causes us to tell ourselves stories we believe validate our emotional reactions and vindicate our judgement and perceived righteousness. We struggle to recognise this as indifference.

Aren't you curious to learn more about who you are?

When we seek to uncover the reality of our soul truth, we become active participants in the resolution of our unconsciousness and the evolution of our consciousness. It's our willingness to be present in the process of evolution that facilitates the recognition of opportunities to resolve what is oppressing our souls.

Some of our worst experiences are the ones that become pivotal to our spiritual growth and soul maturity. Within our worst experiences, it's wise to remember we can be a source of grace and compassion.

- Grace is unconditional love for truth in action; it facilitates the utilisation of the core essences of our souls.

- Grace stems from a choice to accept reality. This allows us to stop fighting reality.

- Grace is the willingness to forgive ourselves, others, and the collective unconsciousness of mankind for our immaturity. Life constantly exposes our immaturity, both collectively and individually.

- Grace provides an opportunity to evolve and flourish.

Grace and compassion enable us to accept and learn from our own soul immaturity. They also lead us to participate in the flow of consciousness—truth, while recognising the learning process.

With regard to spiritual evolution, everyone learns at their own pace. This is a guide to help you contemplate how we learn:

1. First there is a recognition of wanting to expand our awareness, which ignites our thoughts and feelings about something. Even when we cannot explain it, it's an acknowledgement of wanting to understand whatever sparked our curiosity.

This requires us to follow our curiosity.

2. Second is the exploration stage—inquisitiveness about something that allows us to move from wanting to understand, to taking the actions that enable us to explore. We have to confront the barriers that impede the growth of our awareness. We must choose to explore what we are aware of while objectively observing ourselves and reality. This enables us to become self-reflective or mindful of a concept.

This requires honesty and open-mindedness.

3. Third is active participation, engaging in the development of our awareness. It is choosing to build an understanding while recognising we are on an expedition. Honest self-examination—truth-seeking and soul-searching are key. When we are inspired by others' awareness, it's imperative to recognise why we are moved, and crucial to correlate

their information to our own life story. It's vital to trust ourselves to feel so we can discover what resonates within our souls. It's being open to new discoveries, while questioning and challenging beliefs, judgements, fears and control structures.

This requires truthfulness and a willingness to be dynamically engaged with reality.

4. Fourth is dynamic self-awareness. It means acknowledging how we interact with what we are exploring, with others, and ourselves. Recognising our sequenced emotional patterns, reactions, and how we treat others is essential to our soul-exploration process. It is comprehending the importance of retaining what has been revealed and the truth of our awareness. This leads to trusting ourselves to know and feel the difference between conscious and unconscious energy. If we're currently unsure, it means we acknowledge the uncertainty and engage with honesty.

This requires respect for insight, appreciation for the journey of discovery and trust in the process. To maintain the momentum of exploration, we have to examine what is familiar, debunk the illusions of knowing, and embrace the unknown.

5. Fifth is unification with truth, utilising what we have learnt and putting it into practice. Unification is being mindfully aware of choice and choosing to retain the truth discovered while still willing to expand awareness. It is having and valuing our own insight. If there is fraudulence, there is no unification with truth. If we value the significance of truth, we are able to recognise our own indifference to truth, and trigger a conscious response. If we are unable to feel or recognise truth we have embarked on the reconnaissance of our unconscious energy, such as beliefs, images, illusions, or judgement. This will last as long as we want—or until we can no longer tolerate our own indifference, protect our denial, or uphold the control required to fool ourselves.

This requires trustworthiness and the willingness to value truth. It also requires us to embrace our significance, uniqueness, independence, and individuality.

6. Sixth is integration, where the learning becomes part of us. It's instinctual consciousness—evolution in action. If there is fraudulence, integration will not occur. Instead, we will perform from instinctual unconsciousness aimed at protecting beliefs, images, illusions, and judgement.

This requires unconditional love for our souls, truth, and our origins, in addition to trusting our natural instincts.

7. Seventh is continuity. It's a true connection with the value of what has been learnt. Regardless of what we are experiencing, our understanding of the value of truth is at the forefront of how we engage with life and respond to others. If we waver, it is recognised, and we align back with the integrity of our soul. We flow with consciousness, knowing it is our natural essence. This is full integration, which does not mean the end of learning. It means being open to discovering and expanding more awareness. It's living valuing our connection with truth and consciously experiencing evolution.

This requires us to be of our true essence, to live aware, and to be connected with the divinity of who we are.

Learning from our experiences and our relationships with others is crucial to our spiritual evolution. It can be difficult to objectively observe what triggers our emotional reactions and yet vital to developing a strong understanding of ourselves. Spiritual evolution stems from knowing ourselves. Evolution does not occur unless we resolve the unconscious energy that burdens our soul.

We cannot be enlightened if we are anchored to denial.

Learning from life is not a straightforward event, nor is it neat and tidy. It's messy because we are attempting to deal with the irrationality of our emotions as we head towards the unknown. At times learning is a chaotic adventure, and each exploration can highlight more than we bargained for. It's a dynamic, multi-strand journey.

Learning requires us to acknowledge ourselves and reality. Acknowledgement allows us to progress and to expand our awareness.

These are points to consider as you explore your soul truth.
This is a guide to the progression of learning. You are unique, and so is your learning process.

7th Continuity
Being of your truth

6th Intergration
Uncondiltonally
loving your soul,
truth & your origins

5th Unification with truth
Embracing
your uniqueness,
independence & individuality

4th Dynamic self-awareness
Respecting your
insight, curiosity & journey

3rd Active participation
Truthfulness &
engaged with reality

2nd Exploration stage
Honesty &
open mindedness

1st Acknowledgement
Follow your curiosity

CHAPTER SIX
Evolution and Your Core Essences

When we truthfully explore our own energy and resolve what's unresolved, we contribute conscious energy to life. Core essences are different frequencies of conscious energy. Resolution or evolution do not occur without the presence and emanation of our core essences.

It's necessary for us to be truthful to embark on an evolutionary process—journey of discovery. They always require us to utilise our core essences so we can understand and resolve of our unconsciousness. Our core essences are bridges that support us to walk the resolution process towards evolution.

Anything that deprives you of your core essences contributes to your soul oppression.

Core essences flow within our soul's consciousness and are part of our authenticity. Below are the core essences explored in all the Insight & Awareness Anthology. There are many more, and you may want to add to the list:

- *Acceptance*
- *Appreciation*
- *Care*
- *Clarity*
- *Compassion*
- *Dynamism*
- *Freedom*
- *Grace*
- *Harmony*

- *Honesty*
- *Hope*
- *Independence*
- *Individuality*
- *Integrity*
- *Joy*
- *Kindness*
- *Loyalty*
- *Patience*

- *Peace*
- *Purity*
- *Serenity*
- *Trust*
- *Truthfulness*
- *Uniqueness*
- ………………
- ………………
- ………………

We have many experiences that expose the crux of our soul's unconsciousness, before coming to an understanding of the true value of our awareness of truth and our core essences. Each life experience, relationship, and event, ignites a journey into our emotional labyrinth. When we acknowledge the journey, even in hindsight, we build our understanding of ourselves. We strengthen our trust in ourselves to deal with the reality of our soul's unconsciousness, when we are truthful about our emotional reverberations and the way we ricochet from one emotion to the next. This requires objectivity as well as embracing and utilising the energy of our core essences—the authenticity of who we are. When we protect the energy of our soul's unconsciousness, we do not learn and are destined to walk the same paths.

Resolution and evolution are entwined.
The opportunity to experience them is
interlaced with everything
you experience.

We are constantly journeying into the labyrinth of our own creation while experiencing the labyrinth of life, as they are entwined. Our individual journey is interlaced with the converging paths of others and life events; however, it is our individual reactions and responses that lead us to experience the truth of our own labyrinth.

We evolve as our awareness of truth expands. Our awareness expands as we resolve the energy of our soul's unconsciousness. This allows us to trek further into the depths of our soul's unconsciousness, recognising the layers—pathways—we have experienced before. We experience the same path many times, but it changes because of our attitude towards what we know of the path.

When you walk the path, retaining and applying your core essences, your perspective changes, and you recognise the importance of what you're experiencing. Your core essences help you develop the insight to recognise opportunities to resolve and evolve.

The evolutionary process will eventually take us with recognition to the crux of our soul's unconsciousness—the deeply buried emotions, embedded beliefs, and fears—we use to create a false self-definition. These generate energy we have used consistently, but have not recognised the truth or the extent of it. There are many embedded beliefs and fears within the crux of our soul's unconsciousness, and our first reaction is often unconscious and impulsive. We justify and protect them while attempting to vindicate ourselves. This causes us to fortify what is in the crux with whatever unconscious energy we deem useful. It could be manipulation, resentment, deception, defiance, judgement, or pride. However, for these energies to be sustainable, we must align with impenetrable indifference to truth. Impenetrable until we decide to be honest about it.

The crux of our unconsciousness can only be resolved while applying what we have learned to be true and utilising the core essences of our souls. It is essential to value the significance of truth. Otherwise, our compulsion to justify our stance, vindicate ourselves, and protect our unconsciousness can leave us embodying the indifference to ourselves and others.

To have recognition of the crux of our unconsciousness, we need to first resolve the layers of our denial that camouflage the truth of our energy. We also must address our avoidance that protects what is hidden in the crux. This is how we build awareness of the issues that sustain our unconsciousness. The keyword here is recognition. The crux of our soul's unconsciousness influences how we utilise unconscious energy. We have been submissively protecting everything in the crux since we created or aligned with it.

Think of the energy in the crux as the initiators of your separation from being aware of your own soul—false beliefs and misguided fears—that caused you to devalue yourself, to ignore your own insight, and to override your awareness of truth. If we refuse to be honest, we lose insight and focus on having control over our beliefs and fears. This causes us to ricochet within our own soul's unconsciousness, and we get emotionally messy.

When we approach the fears and embedded beliefs within the crux of our soul's unconsciousness with maturity, we can examine them. It is through examination that we realise our fears. Embedded beliefs expose our unconsciousness about the truth of ourselves. Maturity means retaining and applying what we have learned while respecting our soul authenticity. This develops a conscious understanding of our own self-worth and significance. If we lack maturity, we run the gauntlet of the energy of our soul's unconsciousness, building stories to tell ourselves to override the truth of our energy, behaviour, beliefs, and fears. This is how we become lost in our own soul oppression.

Maturity is the result of expanded awareness, insight, and trust in the value of truth. Maturity cannot be faked; images and illusion will be completely undone within the energy of the crux of our soul's unconsciousness. This is why we apply effort to fortifying and protecting the crux. However, this effort also exposes the truth of our own behaviour. It can become an opportunity to examine if we are willing to be truthful with ourselves. We are the pivotal point; we choose how we react and respond to our own energy.

You need to be truthful to resolve,
or you will protect your desired denial by being
indifferent to the reality of your own reactions and responses.

Many will refuse to self-examine and will go straight to defending and fortifying their protection mechanism. This causes them to operate from their desire for control, initiating judgement to secure their position. Their indifference to truth will be strengthened until they believe they are no longer under the threat of facing the truth of their emotional selves. This is particularly strong in narcissists and those who operate comfortably from any of the seven deadly sins. Unfortunately, they are willing to hurt those they love. Even those who have helped them or are completely innocent are caught in the cross-fire of their pursuit for control. This is the part of human nature that shocks us all, as the extent to which they will go often has no boundaries and leaves a trail of pain and betrayal in their wake.

Resolution and evolution are entwined. Whatever we believe we have resolved from within the crux of our unconsciousness, needs to be retained and applied for evolution to emerge.

Our awareness becomes our searchlight looking for truth, and our core essences are our tool kit for the process of resolution and evolution. When we deny truth, abandon our awareness, and disassociate from the significance of our core essences, we catapult ourselves into what is unresolved. We often knowingly repeat what we had previously believed resolved, discarding our awareness. We can immerse ourselves in what we thought was resolved, only to discover what we hid from ourselves in our previous expeditions.

There are layers to each of our unresolved emotions. Our barriers to truth, framework of soul oppression, and the embedded beliefs and fears stored in the crux of our soul's unconsciousness, are all layered with unresolved emotions. It is our denial of our soul's worth that enables us to create the complexities of our unconsciousness. It is knowing our soul worth that enables us to actively participate in our own resolution and evolution.

We created the labyrinth of our soul's unconsciousness, and we have aligned with the energy we produce to sustain the unconsciousness of our souls. We can either choose to secure the oppression of our souls, or to be our own liberators. We can choose to stay present, engaged, and truthful. When we drift into indifference, we have to choose to be truthful: otherwise, we will continue perpetuating and creating the unconsciousness of our souls.

The process of resolution and evolution are entwined and it is a dynamically layered adventure. We are constantly revealing what is unresolved to ourselves, which provides an opportunity to utilise our core essences. Sometimes we lean heavily on trust and patience; other times we require ourselves to acknowledge the value of our significance, uniqueness, independence, and individuality. Each core essence has a unique way of anchoring us to the truth of our soul. However, if we don't value the significance of our core essences, we will be unable to use them to their full capacity.

One of the important parts of the evolutionary process is the willingness to explore what is being revealed. As with all labyrinths, we can never be sure what the next junction or passage will expose to us. We can never presume the process is complete, because resting on our laurels creates stagnation.

Stagnation slows the flow of consciousness within our souls
and inhibits the evolutionary process.
Being present within the truth of our reality wards off stagnation
and enables us to feel the exquisiteness of our soul.

When we accept life as an expedition to explore the truth of our soul, we embrace exploring our unconsciousness, knowing that it creates opportunities for how to embrace our consciousness. *You are the pivotal point; you decide what you acknowledge or deny. You also decide what you embrace or are indifferent to. This means the choices you make are significant to your journey of life.*

When you accept that you are on an evolutionary journey, you realise there are no wrong turns within the labyrinths you encounter, only opportunities. What you miss today, you will experience again. What you resolve today will enable you to approach life through the lens of what you have learnt. This means you grace yourself with an opportunity to evolve beyond the compulsive default mechanisms you use to separate from your awareness of truth. However, when you refuse to value what you can learn from your experiences in life, you default back to cyclic patterns that expose unresolved issues.

Every emotion is layered, and we will experience each layer of our unresolved emotions. Resolution occurs in stages, and as each layer is resolved, it lightens the burden of our soul's unconsciousness. Regardless of what occurs, we are still experiencing an opportunity because it will either reveal the consciousness or unconsciousness of our souls.

Evolution is a process that has no shortcuts. We experience the truth of our own energy, and we have the freedom to choose how to react or respond. At times we will experience the reconnaissance stage of exploring our own energy, and at other times the jigsaw comes together, and we will be in a position to make informed choices. All of this is part of the process and respecting our core essences allows the process to be less traumatic. We traumatise ourselves when we fight against our own awareness, insight, and truth. We may not realise it, but we create shame, fear, and indifference to escape our truth. We oppress ourselves because we elect to deny reality or to protect the illusion of control. The question to ask is: Is it worth the effort and pain we create?

Evolution is complicated by our compulsion to harshly judge ourselves. An essential component of evolution is a willingness to give ourselves grace for being immature. When we forgive ourselves for the creation of our soul's unconsciousness, we embrace taking responsibility for our souls and being accountable for our energy. This enables us to freely walk the unique pathway of our resolution and evolution, while accepting we are naturally significant, unique, individual souls.

When we choose to recognise, acknowledge, and resolve what we created, we free ourselves from the stagnation of our soul oppression. We use our unresolved emotions to create separation from our awareness of our soul and disassociation from feeling our natural resonance with truth.

We choose the value we place on our core essences, and when they are important to us, we change life into a conscious journey of nurturing ourselves back to the truth of who we are. We are the game changer who can walk the path of evolution. However, to truly recognise and acknowledge what life is presenting to us, we must be respectful of our souls.

Evolution is the process of unifying with the truth of your soul.
In the process, you resolve the cause and effect of
your separation from your awareness of truth
and of who you naturally are.

The Voyage

We trek into the crux of the labyrinth,
only to voyage back to the entry, on a similar pathway,
hopefully retaining and applying our new awareness.

If we retain our new awareness
and are prepared to apply what we've learnt,
evolution has occurred.

If we discard the awareness along the journey back to the start,
we have experienced reconnaissance in preparation for
the next voyage back into the crux of the labyrinth.

Evolution only occurs when our awareness becomes insight
and is applied in the way we live.

The crux of the labyrinth will be visited many times
during a true evolutionary journey.

Each fear and embedded belief will beckon the trek.
Some you'll find easy; others will cause you to experience a tidal wave of emotions
that require you to anchor to the truth of yourself, and truly acknowledge
the reality of your experience.

Your anchors to the truth of yourself
are the core essences
of your soul.

Core essences prevent you from drifting into indifference.
They allow you to recognise the horizon beyond the earthy plane.
They assist you in acknowledging the significance of
the evolution of your soul.

Core essences hold you in the flow of your own consciousness.
They provide you with support and stability during the emotional storms
endured within the process of discovery, resolution, and evolution.

Your core essences bring you back to the truth of your soul,
as they form a bridge that enables the voyage of life to be introspective.
They guide you to new awareness and support you in the understanding that follows.
They require you to respect them, so they can be utilised to their full capacity.

You are the pivotal point of the capacity of your own core essences.
How you regard them determines their value.

SECTION 3

Awakening is to be open and inspired by your soul.
It is also an invitation to your origins of truth that you are ready to
attune to the truth of your own significance, uniqueness, individuality, and independence,
so you can consciously unify with who you are and what you are naturally part of.

INVITATION
To Explore Your
Soul & Origins

Chapter Seven
Awakened Consciousness

Consciousness is the energy of the purity of our souls. It is the energy from which our souls are born.

Each soul has a unique frequency that is a strand within the collective consciousness—divinity. Regardless of our individual awareness, the collective consciousness is always aware of each soul. We are anchored to this collective consciousness; we are of divinity—*True Source Divine Origin Consciousness.*

Consciousness is a mystery,
yet it is the fundamental force of our existence.

To be of our own consciousness is to resonate with the energy of our origins, unified with the frequency of our core essences while completely aware of being a soul. When we awaken, we attune, which means we become receptive, aware, and we value the uniqueness of our soul. We also become unified and in harmony with the collective consciousness. We have a relationship with the origins of our soul—the collective consciousness. It is a relationship that we either neglect and abuse, or nurture and respect. We choose how we engage with this relationship.

Understanding the complexities of consciousness may remain a mystery while we experience life on earth in a physical body. It is obvious this is beyond our complete comprehension, and we would be fools to believe otherwise. Consciousness is not aligning to a belief system; it's awakening to the truth we belong to. We have to explore beyond our perceived known to embrace the true essence of our being.

When we accept the individuality of our relationship with *True Source Divine Origin Consciousness* and are prepared to go within ourselves and do the work required to unshackle from our oppression, we awaken to the truth. This means it is no longer a belief; it is a continuous, evolving understanding.

Many of us think attuning and unifying means surrendering to the universe, believing it is a way of awakening our consciousness. However, what does that mean? The statement has merit if it implies, we stop fighting and resisting what was once considered an enemy. This could be our truth, our own authenticity, or our humanity and love. If it is an acceptance of "what is" and leads to an acknowledgment of our own reality, it creates a foundation to develop a true relationship with the flow of consciousness.

Spiritual surrender can be interpreted in so many ways, and there are many who use it as an excuse to relinquish self-responsibility. This means they've missed the mark because spirituality means to take responsibility for accepting the truth. Some also miss the mark, by stating they are surrendering, with the expectation that our origins—the flow of consciousness—will provide them with the life they want.

Surrender means to acknowledge we cannot control life; we can only experience life. Our decisions, energy, and our way of being, influence our life experiences, but it is only part of it. Think of all that contributes to a moment—it is beyond our comprehension.

Imagine life is a game of chess. Life is the board and across from you is truth. The pieces—decisions and actions—cause you to move around the board. However, you are unable to perceive all the moves ahead, but the flow of consciousness is your life coach. It is your support crew, and it tries to advise without taking over. It highlights what will enable you to play to your full potential. Some refer to this life coach or support crew as the *True Source Divine Origin Consciousness*, divinity, the universe, or by the name of a deity. It is constantly providing you with opportunities to live authentically, attuned and unified with the flow of consciousness. You are of this flow, and life and truth are not your opponents. They are teachers—working in harmony—providing emotional and spiritual growth opportunities. Having a sense of belonging to the flow of consciousness is unifying and attuning.

Surrender is an acceptance that we are part of a bigger picture. It is a multilayered chessboard. When we recognise pursuing ultimate control over life comes from a limited understanding, we accept life is beyond our control. This enables us to freely choose to go with the flow, consciously aware of our responsibility to be truthful within our relationship with the consciousness of our soul and all that exists.

Acknowledging we are unconditionally loved and constantly supported by our origins is a move towards freely embracing that we are each an integral part of the expansion of consciousness. Life is constantly providing opportunities to expand our consciousness. Our personal expansion contributes to the expansion of the collective consciousness.

Awakened consciousness is being aware and receptive that we are in a relationship with the essence of our existence—*True Source Divine Origin Consciousness*. Unifying and attuning is becoming a friend to the origins of our soul.

Think of it this way: When you become friends with someone, are you asking them to surrender to you, claim defeat, and allow you to be the authority over them? Or are you hoping to share experiences and build a relationship based on mutual loyalty, equality, and love for one another?

Valued friendships cause us to want to be the best of who we are in each other's presence. It also comes with the responsibility to address whatever causes us to momentarily exploit, ignore, or devalue that friendship. Valued friendships develop from the intent to love, support, and do our utmost to improve the quality of the relationship. This is done by being there and embracing the value, worth, and significance of a relationship. We can have this kind of relationship with *True Source Divine Origin Consciousness*.

The following are concepts to explore:

Consciousness is the fundamental energy of truth. It is fundamental to the truth of:

- Souls—authenticity.

- Our journey and eternalness.

- Our past, present, and future.

- Ourselves in relation to the energy of our surroundings, origins, and our internal world.

- The force that creates and sustains the varying forms of our existence. This includes while within the physical body on earth and when our soul returns to our origins after the death of our body.

Consciousness is the truth flowing, and is present in all that exists. It is irrelevant whether we are aware of it, understand it, or can articulate, label, or describe it. Consciousness is beyond our mankind programming, conditioning, and any indoctrinations used to try and control our awareness of consciousness.

We strive to be aware of our consciousness and attune to the truth of who we fundamentally are at the core of our existence. We are naturally of consciousness and seek awareness of and unification with this truth.

> *Awakened consciousness is being aware and in the flow of your truth.*

Awakened consciousness is to flow with the purity of our souls and with truth. It stems from valuing our awareness and relationship with truth: the truth of reality, truth of our origins, and truth of ourselves. It is being truly honest about the entirety of our own awareness.

> *Being honest about what you are aware of, even if you do not understand it yet, enables your awareness to expand.*
> *This means you are consciously participating in creating an environment within Yourself that allows insight, intuition, and truthfulness to be the catalyst of the expansion of your awareness of your consciousness.*

The flow of consciousness is within the core of our souls. It is from this flow that we emanate our core essences. (See Chapter 6—Evolution and Your Core Essences).

True Source Divine Origin Consciousness

The flow of consciousness is multi-strands of energy that descend from our anchor in our origins, which flows through the core of our being. Each strand is nurturing our soul. Once it has reached the furthest recess of our separation from the truth of our soul, it ascends, returning to our origin. It's a continuous cycle of unique frequencies—strands of consciousness—that flow through you, from the collective consciousness. It is the life force of our existence—the true essence of our soul.

We are anchored to our origins. *There is a part of your soul's consciousness that still resides in the collective consciousness of truth—your origins.* Our soul retains this knowledge and connection. This is what we endeavour to unify with. Awakened consciousness is being aware and attuned to the unification, integration, and the continuity of our souls within the flow of consciousness.

We awaken to our consciousness. It has always been, at our core, the fundamental energy of our existence and is only discovered when truth is valued and embraced. Awakened consciousness stems from embracing our direct connection to the origins of truth, life, and reality. We are part of the origins of all that exists. Embracement only occurs through the mutual exchange of unconditional love, which is the gateway. Imitation or hidden agendas halt our embrace of consciousness, while consciousness is always ready to embrace.

Awakened consciousness is embracement of consciousness. It is enthusiastic acceptance, and a willingness to share ourselves and to be an expression of love. Awakened consciousness is not only the intent to acknowledge, reside, unify, and flow with the energy of truth. It's to be as one and this requires us to be of our truth. It is the actualisation of the intent to be pure-hearted in our love for ourselves, each other, and all that exists. The clearer we are in our intent, the easier it is to embrace the energy of our origins.

The flow of consciousness is without separation or fragmentation—it is pure and authentic. We create an illusion of being separated from truth, our origins, and from the truth of ourselves. In the illusion, we actively generate thoughts, control structures, avenues of indifference, beliefs, fears, and retain our unresolved emotions, all of which create further separation from our awareness of our consciousness. We store and carry fragmented energy—unconscious energy—that is vibrating below the frequency of truth.

We burden ourselves with the unconscious energy we create that cannot reside in the purity of truth. We use this unconscious energy to sustain separation from our awareness of ourselves, truth, reality, and our relationship with our origins. This fragmentation of energy is the energy of our soul's unconsciousness.

Resolution and evolution are processes that lead us to become aware of our separation from truth. Resolving what creates the separation and then unifying with truth are the processes of evolving our awareness and understanding of our consciousness. It is recognising the eternal reality of being a soul and choosing to flow with the energy of our soul's consciousness.

Our perception of consciousness is limited by our beliefs; however, our consciousness is limitless. We struggle to comprehend the creative force of consciousness. We don't fully understand the potential of our souls, origins, and truth, so we create beliefs about consciousness to pacify ourselves or to create a quest for enlightenment. However, we often lose awareness of the initial spark of curiosity that awakened us to the realisation that there is more to learn about ourselves. We can turn consciousness into a pursuit to achieve, instead of being truthful with ourselves and allowing our awareness of consciousness to expand.

Awakened consciousness is to be present in what is occurring, to feel the multi-strands of truth converging that create a point of interest for us to experience or objectively observe. All our senses react to our awareness of the multi-strands of truth.

How we experience the same point will differ when our awareness is separated from the flow of consciousness.

How we experience the same point will differ when we are awakened to, aware of, and unified with the flow of consciousness. We feel the uniqueness of our soul as energy communing with the strands of truth within the experience. However, what we have is shared knowledge, resonance, and awareness of the true frequency of this energy. This is difficult to articulate and is communicated through a language beyond words. It is a soul-to-soul connection. This is often experienced with a knowing look while feeling the pristine frequency of truth.

> *To be in the flow of consciousness is to*
> *experience the feelings that are beyond beliefs.*
> *It is an awareness of truth and a knowing that*
> *you are of the same energy as truth.*

Awakened consciousness results from being attuned to our soul instinct. Our soul instinct is not learned behaviour; it is our natural response—an internal knowing. We don't learn to be of our consciousness; we awaken to it. We strip away all that impedes the true nature of who we are and create the space to attune with our own consciousness.

Resolving unconscious energy—the fragments of our disharmony with the consciousness of our soul—and evolving an understanding of conscious energy is a stripping away process. Spirituality is the acknowledgement of being on the journey of self-discovery. Evolution is the expansion of understanding and the adaptation to what is uncovered, learned and understood. These are required to advance the quality of our life experiences. Spirituality and evolution lead to awakened consciousness.

Our soul's consciousness is a stream of truth energy—our divinity—that contributes to the river of consciousness that flows through all that exists as it returns to the sea of truth. *True Source Divine Origin Consciousness* is the sea of truth—the collective energy of our origins.

Our soul instinct enables us to recognise truth and resonates with the frequency of truth. We instinctively know the value and significance of being freely attuned with truth. Being awakened is to freely attune to the pure frequency of our souls and our origins—collective of divine consciousness.

Attuned with truth means:

- Unity.

- To love.

- To be in harmony.

- To be sensitive to and aware of truth.

- To be at one with truth and aware of the connection.

- Dynamically adapting to reality without losing integrity.

- To understand and be appreciative of the virtues of truth.

- A sympathetic relationship—one of mutual trust and understanding.

- To voluntarily be in an accord with truth—an agreeable relationship.

- Being able to perceive and recognise the frequency, value, and significance of truth.

- A responsive relationship—one of acknowledgement, respect, value, and receptiveness.

- Acknowledge what your personal views are ………………………………………

………………………………………………………………………………………

………………………………………………………………………………………

Awakened consciousness is to be awakened to our relationship with truth, the divinity of our souls, and of our origins. It is knowing, loving, and accepting the reality of being a strand within a greater mass.

Awakening to our consciousness stems from a willingness to acknowledge our awareness of the entirety of both our conscious and unconscious energy. It is to be aware of the different energies that interconnect in the dance of life that creates an opportunity to evolve our souls and our awareness of who we naturally are.

***Awakened consciousness is remembering who we are
and what we are part of.***

We are a stream that leads to a river that feeds the sea.
The sea is holding the direction to travel, and a journey
is required before the sea can be accessed.
The sea awaits our conscious return.

If we do not return consciously and instead return with the
mud of our denial and stench of indifference, we are reincarnated,
and another journey occurs, until we are the
pristine water of our origins.

We are a stream of uniqueness, authenticity, and independence that
can choose to freely attune to our origins of truth, accepting the
significance of being part of the sea of truth.

CHAPTER EIGHT
Significance

Sometimes we need to be reminded of our significance. We are prone to losing awareness of how each of us are significant to the origins of truth, our souls, and the tapestry of life.

We are part of existence. *Now that is something to ponder.* We are part of the mystery of life. Our experiences, reactions, and emanations matter. Our energy contributes to the collective energy of life. Our resolution of unconscious energy—unresolved emotions, control structures, false beliefs, fears—removes unconscious energy from the energetic mass energy of mankind—our collective unconsciousness. What we resolve enables the flow of consciousness space to expand.

We forget the importance of our existence and deny ourselves the recognition of our own significance. We confuse significance with success, notoriety, and external validation. However, significance stems from knowing we are of worth, regardless of our approval rating, finances, position, body image, or life experiences.

Knowing we are significant is recognition of the meaningfulness of our existence, even when we haven't fully comprehended what that means. There is purpose to our lives, and our denial of this leaves us dumbing ourselves down. Knowing that we are significant is not an invitation to excuse narcissism, to be arrogant, or to feel superior to others. As we realise the natural significance of our own existence, we become awakened to the significance of all that exists.

We are always significant; what we lose is awareness of this fact. We lose awareness because we focus on how others have treated us that left us feeling insignificant. When we have experienced another's indifference towards the truth of who we are, it triggers reactions that can lead to the construction of beliefs of insignificance—not being good enough.

A sense of insignificance can be derived from shame, fear, insecurity, and negative beliefs about ourselves that others can use as a way into our psyche. People who delight in rendering another as insignificant build a false foundation and scaffold the illusion of controlled significance. Controlled significance means they get to dictate why they are significant, instead of accepting the natural significance of all. As superior as they believe they are, they have missed the mark of true significance. They do not know themselves or what they are part of. So, how can they form an accurate opinion of another?

Significance is felt when we trust ourselves to be of truth and accept we have natural value. When we have accepted that we are part of the flow of consciousness, our significance becomes more apparent.

When we trust all that exists is significant,
it inspires us to nurture our souls.

When we operate from, and emanate the core essences of our souls, there is a feeling of freedom. It is natural, often done without thought or recognition—it is instinctive. The freedom to be of our truth and to flow unified with the consciousness within ourselves and in our life experiences ignites an internal knowing of our significance. Unfortunately, because we fear each other, we have deprived ourselves of an environment conducive to where this feels natural. We have superimposed systems, judgments, competitions, and pecking orders that led us to fear being judged, humiliated, shamed, rejected, and discarded. When we are separated from our truth, what we create we superimpose over our natural way of being. This leaves us operating from the unconscious energy we store and carry.

We have become fearful of being vulnerable to each other's unconsciousness. This caused us to devalue our own significance. Enlightenment means "to know thy self". It's not the result of others' approval, following a trend, or submitting to power and control. Enlightenment is recognising we are significant, and unification with truth is dependent on us remembering who we are and what we are naturally part of. We are of truth and born significant.

When we devalue ourselves and discount the importance of our origins, it is easy for fear to replace our awareness of our own significance. This causes us to want reassurance. Our fear of being classed as insignificant has caused us to cower in a herd mentality. This causes us to forsake the equality of all souls, and we no longer see each other as a collective of individuals—as humanity. We look upon ourselves as different herds of mankind, and history has proven this causes pain and trauma to perpetuate.

We only see others as insignificant when we are indifferent. When we are indifferent to our own humanity we lose awareness of our souls. Indifference demoralises the significance of our uniqueness, independence, and individuality. It is our recognition of, and respect for our uniqueness, independence, and individuality that enables us to embrace our significance.

The fear of the magnitude of our significance has us frightened and retreating from the true impact our energy has on reality. We have conditioned ourselves to deny the significance of being aware of our own energy. We collectively downplay the importance of our feelings and emotions, and we fixate on judgement, manipulation, and control.

Respecting awareness enables us to discover, explore, and embrace our own truth. Our fear of the magnitude of the value and significance of our souls has us fighting against, and oppressing the truth of our internal knowing and core essences. Our unwillingness to be completely honest with ourselves and each other impedes our soul instinct.

Acknowledging our significance enables us to recognise the importance of how we interact with all that exists. When we allow ourselves to flow in the consciousness of our souls, emanating the core essences of who we naturally are, our interactions become arenas for significance to be a shared experience.

When we express our core essences, we feel freedom. Core essences are an expression of our true nature unimpeded by soul-oppressive energy, beliefs, and fears. When we express the truth of our souls, we enable ourselves to feel freedom from our soul oppression—free of the burden of the energy of our soul's unconsciousness that we have not resolved and evolved from yet. The freedom felt is a spark of recognition of the significance of our souls and of our interaction with each other. It is an undefinable energy, yet we instinctively recognise it, especially when we are aware of its existence.

- When we feel *joyful, freedom* is felt and becomes an invitation for others to join in.

- When we are miserable, we lose our awareness of our freedom of choice.

- When we are *kind, freedom* is felt and becomes an acknowledgement of each other's true value.

- When we are cruel, freedom is lost, and we become a slave to the ramifications of our cruelty.

- When we express our *unconditional love, freedom* is felt and encouraged.

- When indifference reigns, freedom is oppressed for both the perpetrator and victim.

We may not realise the true significance of expressing our core essences, but the significance of our existence is very evident in those who appreciate being on the receiving end of them. Being of our core essences is sharing the truth of our soul.

We may recognise the significance of what we do and ignore the significance of who we are. The more we are aware of our willingness to feel or express our truth freely to ourselves, the more we realise the significance of our *being*. Being stems from an awareness of our own existence and presence in the reality of what we are experiencing.

Being is choosing to share the truth of our souls. It is majorly significant when we turn up and are present. If you are unsure, ask a five-year-old at a school play whose parents are in the crowd or a patient in hospital whose family and friends have arrived. You may remember a time you needed a hug of reassurance, and someone gave you that hug. It is not all about the action. It's the feeling of support, being valued and significant enough for another to share in your experience. This is felt if they are present. The action alone does not induce the feeling of soul connection; they have to be willing to share the truth of their soul. We are human beings, not human doings.

When we are willing to feel or express our truth freely to ourselves, we naturally feel the significance of truth and from there we can feel our own significance. Truth and our acceptance of truth illuminates the true nature of our significance.

When our soul's essence is free to flow, there is a resonance with truth that infiltrates the soul-oppressive energy—such as judgement, resentment, or shame—that we use to define ourselves. Being aware and present within the infiltration changes how we perceive many of the beliefs, fears, and unresolved emotions that plague our perceptions of ourselves.

Significance is a feeling of being present and aware,
expressing truth, and acknowledging our presence.

Our significance is felt strongly when we are our authentic selves, emanating and trusting our soul instinct to share our truth. Sharing is giving freely with no hidden agenda. Sharing our truth is being. If another is fortunate to be present and to resonate with the truth of our energy, our presence will be naturally significant to them. This could be for a fleeting moment, but it is felt, and it cannot be owned, replicated, orchestrated, or controlled. When another acknowledges our significance, it is because they have been present, shared the same space, and felt the essence of our natural being.

You are a significant, unique, independent, individual soul of
True Source Divine Origin Consciousness,
who has ventured into this world to expand your awareness of yourself and truth.
You are an opportunity for the expansion of awakened consciousness;
you are an opportunity for evolution.

CHAPTER NINE
Karma

K arma means action. Every decision, reaction, and response to our life situations and internal reality is an action. The energy we generate from our soul's unconsciousness, or emanate from our soul's consciousness, stems from an action. A decision is an action. Thoughts, spoken words, behaviours, and deeds are actions that generate energy. Our feelings and emotions are different types of energy—an action.

Karma is the law of cause and effect. What we do, say, and even think has a cause and effect as we create energy. This energy contributes to our life experiences. It contributes to our relationship with ourselves, others, life, and our origins of truth.

> *When we talk of karma, we are talking about*
> *responsibility and accountability for our own energy.*
> *We are the creators of our energy, which has a*
> *cause and effect on our souls and life.*

We are energy creators, and we have the freewill to decide the type of energy we create. We create an environment that fosters either conscious or unconscious energy. Our creations have a cause and effect. They have purpose, intent, and consequences.

We are responsible for the following:

- The purpose—the reason why we do what we do. The goal we wish to achieve and the result we strive for.

- The intent—the energy we want to put in motion. The stepping-stones to what we mean to do, whether we achieve it or not. How we think and want things to play out. What we believe will provide us with what we want to happen—what we are prepared to forsake in our attempts to achieve our desires.

- The consequences—the wake of our actions. That which follows—sequenced ramifications.

We are responsible for the purpose and intent behind the energy we create, utilise and exert. True purpose or intent is not necessarily what we say is our purpose or intent; the energy we use is our intent. If we say we want to help someone, because we want to improve our image so we can impress others, our energy reflects our purpose. The intent is manipulation of others to be impressed, not to help, that might be a by-product as it is how we believe we can achieve what we want. However, it will lack the genuineness of kindness, compassion, and integrity.

When what we say, think, and do are not unified, we are utilising a type of unconscious energy. If our true intent stems from the core essences of our souls, our purpose, intent, behaviour and actions are unified, which means we are emanating conscious energy.

Our purpose and intent exude our energy.
Our energy is our presence on earth.

- Energy unified with the consciousness of our soul is conscious energy.

- Unconscious energy is not unified with the consciousness of our soul.

- Both have a cause and effect on how we experience life. We are a presence on earth, and we are the interface of both conscious and unconscious energy.

When we create unconscious energy, we burden our souls with energy that is not of the frequency of truth. This burden is the layers of unconscious energy that constitutes our soul's unconsciousness.

We are responsible for our own creations, and any energy created always returns to the creator. Our thoughts, behaviour, words, and deeds are our creations, and we are responsible for the energy created. We are responsible not only for our own creation of energy, but also our reactions and responses to what others create, share, or inflict.

The more honest and soul mature, the more measured we are in our responses. Soul maturity means we are aware of the purpose, intent, and consequences of our actions, and we make decisions based on this awareness. However, not all consequences are foreseeable and may stray from the original intent and purpose if we or others, do not align with or respect the initial intent.

- Actions can start with *conscious* intent and end up with *unconscious* consequences.

- Actions can start with *unconscious* intent and end up with *conscious* consequences.

Each decision is a juncture of the possibility of conscious or unconscious energy. We are emotional beings and our awareness of, and the way we value truth is highlighted in our decision-making. It's easy to devalue truth and slide into unconscious emotional reactions. This is often done without consideration, we drift into the familiarity of our unconsciousness, but it also dredges up unconscious energy for us to acknowledge. Or we can deliberately choose to devalue truth and purposely align with our unconsciousness, feeding an agenda we have determined is possible to achieve. Our desire for control can take over, and we can become oppositional to all that inhibits us from getting what we want. This is ego driven.

Deciding to do nothing is a response—an action. We are responsible for the energy and consequences we create with our complacency and disengagement from reality.

Our unconscious energy becomes our carried karma. It is energy that returns to us and, if left undealt with, is suppressed and stored in our soul's unconsciousness.

Consequences educate us about the truth of energy, especially our own energy. When we acknowledge the cause and effect of our own actions, both internally and externally, we understand the importance of what we contribute to our reality. For example, pretending to be loving while manipulating others means the truth of our contribution is manipulation and pretence. Karma refers to the truth of an energy, purpose, and intent.

Karma is the truth of our energy;
it is what we decide to create.

Many unforeseen consequences happen because we don't understand the truth of the energy we use. When we react with or are the instigators of unconscious energy—such as resentment, indifference, or spite—we initiate a chain reaction. All who encounter that energy will have a response. This is the same for conscious energy, such as unconditional love, kindness, or truthfulness.

The initial events of unconscious energy may not be your fault, but your reaction to it is your responsibility. When you understand the impact of unconscious energy to your own soul and others, and are willing to value truth, you begin to realise taking responsibility for your energy is part of the evolutionary process. Your truthfulness about yourself leads to evolving beyond the limitations created by unconscious energy.

Others' unconscious reactions to your conscious energy are not your fault, but your reaction to their unconscious reaction is your responsibility. Their unconsciousness should never be an invitation to devalue yourself or the true purpose and intent of your conscious energy. It is not easy to do, because the rejection of your conscious energy— true expressions of your soul—hurts and often leaves you feeling betrayed or discarded. If you have a momentary unconscious reaction but address it with truthfulness, it doesn't become unconscious energy you carry.

Time varies as to how long it takes to address our unconscious reactions. It may take minutes, hours, days, weeks, months, or even years. You carry this energy until it's addressed. Sometimes the awareness of it is there, but you don't know how to deal with it. This means you are in the process of working it out, unwilling to store, suppress, and forget. Your inability to sustain your denial allows your soul's consciousness to cleverly steer you in the direction of finding the required missing pieces. It's not just about that one reaction; it's about what was stored within that created the reaction in the first place.

Applied truthfulness enables a moment of reaction to be felt and acknowledged. You can then thoughtfully participate in the process of self-actualisation, returning to the essence of who you are. Applied truthfulness is valuing the truth of what occurred and making decisions that involve your awareness of truth.

We carry the energy we create, which cannot reside in our consciousness. Our creation of unconscious energy returns to us, and we store it until we are ready to honestly deal with the unconsciousness of our creations. This is the energy of our soul's unconsciousness. It is the legacy of the energy we have created that is indifferent to truth.

Karma has become a word synonymous with carrying the burden of our unconscious energy. The longer we carry the unconscious energy and deny responsibility for it, the more entrenched it becomes in our system. This creates beliefs, fears, and emotional behavioural patterns. The longer we deny our emotional reality, the more impact it has on our awareness of our own soul.

Unconscious energy is energy generated from and stored in our soul's unconsciousness:

- Unresolved emotions
- Embedded beliefs
- Fears
- Control structures

- Barriers to truth
- Framework of soul oppression
- The seven deadly sins
- ………………………………...

*For more information, see Overview of Your Energetic System

For example, if we don't deal with our resentment, we become resentful. It becomes the source of many fears and beliefs that become embedded. This results in emotional patterns we justify while ignoring the truth of our bitterness. We carry it until we resolve our anger. In some cases, what we originally resented becomes irrelevant, as we embody the energy of resentment and develop ways of being indiscriminately indignant. Resentment becomes a burden to our soul and morphs into part of our self-definition, which impedes our process of evolution, soul maturity, and spiritual growth.

What we don't acknowledge or resolve, we become.

The longer we carry the unconscious energy, the more separated we become from the truth. It is within this separation that we keep creating more unconscious energy that is sourced from the original emotional reaction. The original thought, reason for the unresolved emotion, fear or embedded belief, may become lost but the energy resides within until resolved. We don't always have to acknowledge the original creation of the unconscious energy, but we do have to resolve our denial of our own energy in order to resolve the unconscious energy we carry and react from.

The following are concepts to contemplate:

- We react from the initial unconscious energy but lose awareness as to why we sustain it.

  We react from the initial resentment but lose awareness as to why we have chosen to sustain being resentful. We often refuse to contemplate the purpose of carrying this unconscious energy. The event that made us resentful, is not forgotten, but we overlook what we are doing to ourselves with our resentment.

- We protect and defend the effect of unconscious energy but deny the cause.

  We protect and defend our resentfulness, but often deny the cause, unwilling to admit the pain and hurt we felt initially and continue to feel. We'll rehash events to ensure we feel justified in our emotional reactions. Unaddressed issues are displayed in reactions, and we often perpetuate the pattern of protecting and defending our reactions, without addressing the cause of them.

- We become unaware of the reality of our own unconscious energy, because we want to deny responsibility for what we created and still utilise.

  We become unaware of the reality of our resentment, because we want to deny responsibility for it and how we use it to remain emotionally trapped. We become unaware of the different energies we use to sustain the resentment—blame, anger, regret or .... We fear that those who incited our resentment will win, if we don't sustain the energy.

The only way to evolve and awaken to our consciousness is to honestly deal with the reality of our soul's unconsciousness—our karma. Awakened consciousness is unification with the consciousness of our soul, which is only possible through truthfulness.

If you lie about the energy within your soul's unconsciousness, you will be unable to fully reside in the consciousness of your soul. Evolution is a process of discovering the reality of your unconsciousness, learning about the truth of the energy within it, developing a conscious understanding of it, and then deciding to no longer fuel and feed the unconscious energy that burdens your soul. Being of the purity of your soul stems from resolving what is already stored, using your awareness to evolve into the emanation of your consciousness.

It is easy for us to create and perpetuate our unconscious energy. It is labelled unconscious because we are often ignorant to the reality of it, and are willing to use it thoughtlessly. When we strive to be of the purity of our souls, we must be truthful about what we know.

If you are aware that you are operating from unconscious energy—unresolved emotions—acknowledge it. Then accept it as an opportunity to do better, utilise your awareness to steer your behaviour. Every time you don't use your unconscious energy, you are strengthening your connection to your consciousness. If you are aware that you are operating from unconscious energy, and continue to do so, it is intentional. This means you are strengthening your connection to your unconsciousness. Evolution occurs as you knowingly strengthen your connection to your soul.

We have to forgive ourselves for our unconsciousness, or we'll get stuck in our past, beating ourselves up for being unconscious. However, this is similar to yelling at a newborn because he or she cannot walk. Evolution stems from actions, built on new understanding. As we accept, we are in a learning process, we must also accept our history is full of events that stemmed from our lack of understanding. When we learnt to walk, we walked. Whatever we learn—come to understand—must be used, if we want to keep evolving.

Lack of Understanding Story

Jeffery and Dahlia have been married for over thirty years and both are well-renowned marriage counsellors. They have a thriving business. They are also spiritually orientated and have attended retreats with many famous spiritual teachers and self-help gurus. However, they fell into the trap of believing they had evolved, and were unaware of the unconscious energy they utilise to uphold their beliefs. They both focused on sticking to the rules they had inherited from the courses they attended.

They both believed they understood themselves and each other. Their expectations were high about how they should be perceived, and how they must display their wisdom in all their behaviours. What they failed to recognise, or acknowledge were their feelings.

They both refused to let anything challenge their perceptions of how they live, or interrupt their strict regimen of daily practices.

One of their oldest friends, Jackson, came for a visit and as they sat around the dining room table, he noticed how numb they felt. He couldn't help noticing that they seemed robotic. They were very philosophical in their responses, but they were distant and disconnected.

They were keen to talk of Jackson's issues, to delve deep into his emotions, but he refused to go there. "This is a visit, not a session, relax you are not at work now," he protested.

Jeffery began to lecture Jackson on the virtues of inner-work; it bizarrely turned into a forty-five-minute polite rant, while Dahlia continually nodded her head.

Jackson started to laugh, "What are you guys doing? You are saying a lot but it sounds like you're reciting one of your brochures."

"How are your children going, what are they up to?" queried Jackson trying to change the course of the conversation.

"We don't see them much anymore. It's fine, we know it's our time to share with others. It's how it's meant to be. It gives us the space to do what we are trained to do. We are needed elsewhere," proclaimed Dahlia.

Jackson pondered for a second, "What are you trained to do?"

"We are here on Earth to assist others in having stronger relationships, ones of meaning. We are here to educate them on how to live a better life and strengthen their connection with those they love and with themselves," declared Dahlia, half-smiling but with sad eyes.

Jackson gently replied, "Like the one you are having with your children?"

Jeffery interjected, "They are on a different path to us, they are loved, but they find us difficult to be around, because they too refuse to do the inner-work required to deeply connect. They ring occasionally."

Jackson felt sorrow and wondered what had happened to the family.

"How do you feel about your relationship with the children, I know they are grown, but you must miss them?" questioned Jackson.

"Our son only lives two blocks away, but we haven't seen him for months. I don't let myself think about it." Dahlia looked blankly at Jackson, then said, "Please, don't judge us!"

"I'm not, but something is wrong. Isn't he someone you should want a strong connection with? I don't want to be rude, but you both seem distant and numb. I'm not sure who I'm talking to, a person or a lecturer," Jackson timidly announced.

He watched as Jeffery and Dahlia sat silently, looking at each other. Then he asked, "When you first started on your path, what did you learn about yourself?"

Jeffery exhaled deeply, "I first had to address my selfishness and my inability to accept that others can have a different opinion. I used to argue my point. Now, I recognise convincing others to agree with me is a waste of time. I breathe deeply and move on. It's a valuable lesson."

"Is that what you are doing to your children? They don't agree with you, so you moved on. That sounds a bit selfish. You should listen to them. They probably miss you! You would have to agree, having a good relationship with them is important," Jackson said with empathy.

With a deep breath, Jeffery announced it was time for bed and left the table. As he walked away, he commented that he knew Jackson meant well, but didn't understand that he must stay true to his own path.

Jackson sat perplexed by Jeffery's reaction and then asked Dahlia, "When you first started on your path, what did you learn about yourself?"

She smiled, "To not always agree with Jeffery, just to keep the peace, and to think for myself. To be aware of how I suppress my feelings and the importance of communicating them."

"How do you feel about your relationship with the children? I mean feel, not the story you tell yourself," he asked in a curious tone.

"I'm distressed, shattered! I don't know how it has happened. They can't get away from us quick enough, they do the holidays but the laughter is gone," she replied with a sigh of relief. "I don't know who to talk to, or what to do. I have held back my tears, because I knew when you said we were distant that is what our children must feel. We have become so focused on educating others that we have neglected our own family."

Jackson smiled, "If I was your client in the same situation as you, what would you say to me?"

Dahlia put her head down as she ran her hands through her hair. After a moment of deep reflection, she said, "Experts need to learn too, knowledge is ineffectual unless the understanding is applied. It's time to assess your priorities and to voice what you feel. Look at the emotional patterns that stop you from expressing your feelings."

Jackson calmly said, "I think you guys need to talk about how you feel and go visit your children. People drift away from one another, if they don't communicate honestly."

Dahlia half-smiled and replied, "You know we have visited their homes once and have left the onus on them to reach out to us. I have never told them I wanted to spend more time together. I think we have been selfish parents. Thanks, Jackson, I needed that wake-up call."

That was the end of the evening and breakfast was polite exchanges about the weather.

What is unfortunate in this story, is that Dahlia and Jeffery have a wealth of knowledge. They have learned concepts, and have inadvertently disengaged from the truth of their feelings. They are doing, not being. The outside world is taking precedence over their inner world, and they stubbornly refuse to address their own deep issues.

Dahlia and Jeffery are relying on their unconscious energy, such as avoidance, disassociating from their feelings, and masking reality with the concepts they use to disconnect from the truth, to sustain their beliefs of being conscious.

What they have set out to understand has become lost in their desire to secure their own beliefs. The suppression of their emotions, and rejection of what they internally feel is causing them to lie to themselves. They are losing their sense of self, and aligning with what they believe proves they are spiritually evolved and living their soul purpose.

Sometimes it is hard to see the forest if we only look at one tree, or try to carve the tree into what we want to see. Awakened consciousness is the willingness to acknowledge the entirety, objectively looking at and exploring the forest.

We can put Christmas lights on a tree, change its appearance and its purpose, but it's still a tree. This is the same for our unconscious energy—unresolved emotions—we can conceal them, but they will still be there, hidden under the camouflage. We may change their purpose, but not the energy.

Evolution is the process of taking what is hidden and truthfully dealing with it, regardless of whether we have just started our journey or we are a spiritual veteran. Self-discovery is an on-going process, one that requires us to be aware of ourselves—our behaviour, the motives behind our decisions, and how we interact with each other.

Karma Provides Evolutionary Opportunities

When we refuse to engage in the evolutionary process, we create an evolutionary idle. This is where we repetitively experience the energy of our soul's unconsciousness—cycle after cycle. We can experience lifetime after lifetime—in the same energy, until we decide to attentively participate in the resolution of unconscious energy.

Think of evolutionary idle as similar to when you are in a car with the motor running, but you're not going anywhere; you are idling. You want to go somewhere, but you're not doing what is required to create movement, such as taking off the brakes, putting the engine into gear, and pressing your foot on the accelerator. Evolution requires you to find the brakes and then release them. To understand the gear system so you can use it to create movement and to trust yourself to put your foot down on the accelerator, so you keep expanding your awareness.

Our soul's unconsciousness is our energetic storehouse for the consequences of our actions that created, generated and enables us to utilise unconscious energy. It is the energy we create while we are separated from our awareness of our soul that sustains the separation, because it is energy that does not unify with the frequency of truth. It vibrates unconsciously.

- Our conscious energy is of the frequency of truth.

- Our unconscious energy is the vibration of being in denial or indifferent to truth.

Karma is not a trading system where we do a good deed to offset a bad deed, nor is it a reward or a punishment system. It is soul accountability for our creations and an opportunity to learn from our life experiences.

Karma is not an excuse for or a reason why we experienced tragedy, abuse, or exploitation. Life on earth is a freewill arena. We choose how to utilise our freewill. We will experience the energy within our soul's unconsciousness as evolutionary opportunities. How we react to life events and the deeds we enact stem from a choice. We can deal with our previous creations of energy or act them out again. How we act them out is a result of the decision to do so.

There are many undeserving souls who, through no fault of their own, experience the harshest of others' unconscious creations. It's our responsibility to learn from these experiences. We collectively decide what is tolerated, what we ignore, and the value of truth. We do this under our political and judicial systems. These systems should represent what we value and accept as decent human relations. Our collective responsibility is to acknowledge the truth of our history and of our present, because denial does not create growth, nor does it create harmony between souls.

The decisions we make are actions that produce energy, both individually and collectively. When the energy is unconscious it's carried until converted into energy that can flow with consciousness. Truth is required. When we defiantly deny the truth of our history or atrocities, the unconscious energy remains influential until the truth is exposed and acknowledged. If we do not learn from these mistakes, we are destined to repeat them, creating another opportunity to learn about the reality of the energy we create, utilise, and ignore.

When we emanate the core essences of our souls, operating from the purity of who we are, our energy unifies and flows with the ever-present consciousness of truth. The energy flows, and there are consequences to the presence of conscious energy—there is a cause and effect. Others may have an unexpected reaction to conscious energy. It is not always appreciated or embraced. However, this doesn't diminish the significance of it. When conscious energy is met with conscious energy, we experience a soul to soul moment.

Think of it this way. When kindness is met with gratitude and truthfulness, it strengthens the flow of consciousness in that shared moment. It is undeniably felt, and nurtures the soul of both the giver and receiver.

Conscious energy is not stored within our systems, it continues to flow. Conscious energy is never stagnant. It is an expression of our truth and internal unification with the frequency of truth.

We feel this most strongly through unconditional love, especially agenda-free experiences. We experience this upon meeting our newborn babies. Our unconditional love flows, creating an unforgettable moment. This action triggers an awareness of other conscious energy, such as compassion, serenity, hope, and joy. The consequences of these energies enhance and support our evolution.

We are responsible for the conversion of our own creations of unconscious energy into awakened consciousness. We evolve as we understand the energy we unconsciously or deliberately created that cannot reside in the purity of our souls. When we accept that we are creators and participants in an evolutionary process, the law of cause and effect works to our favour. It is not as simple as good and bad, positive and negative, or wrong and right. Our purpose, intent, and willingness to be truthful, all play a part in what we store in the unconsciousness of our souls. When we accept responsibility and accountability for our own energy, we become more aware of the purpose and intent motivating our decisions.

Everything is not a direct link to what we have already stored in our soul's unconsciousness. We have freewill and can create new unconscious energy at any time. Even after we've previously resolved what has been stored from our past, if we elect to use and protect that unconscious energy, we carry it again until it's resolved and we evolve from it.

We are creators with freewill, and we decide what we create.
Our creations are our karma.

Karma is not an excuse to be obnoxious to each other. Acting out our karma so we can free ourselves of our karmic debt, is a lie to justify being unaccountable for our own energy, behaviour, words, and the consequences of our decisions.

We each start life anew. The unconscious energy from previous lives is still in effect, because it is carried until resolved. We experience the energy, but it is never an excuse to act out unconscious energy. That is what occurs but it is not an excuse. We act it out because we haven't chosen to deal with it honestly. Denying responsibility for it— ignoring its impact and being indifferent to the purpose, intent, and consequences— leaves us in an evolutionary idle and a world full of created despair, hurt, and confusion. Unfortunately, innocent people get caught in the crossfire, and they are left having to take responsibility for their reactions to the unconsciousness in others.

Recognising our own unconscious energy, our intent,
and our willingness to deal with reality,
is soul maturity.

The perpetuation of unconscious energy is a cycle only broken by those who take responsibility for their own energy, reactions, and responses. They are the front-runners for the evolution of our collective unconsciousness.

If someone decides to act out what they have stored in their unconsciousness and have decided to expel their energy on you, you may learn something from the experience, but it does not mean you deserved it. It may trigger some of your stored unconscious energy, you can then use this as an opportunity to comprehend the truth of your own energy, but that wasn't their purpose or intent. Through being truthful about yourself, you create the consequence of having a deeper understanding of yourself, but that has nothing to do with them.

Not everything you experience you attract nor is it a mirrored reflection of you. Sometimes it coincides with this, and other times you are the innocent bystander to another's decision to unleash their unconsciousness.

As your awareness builds, you can feel the weight of the world's unconsciousness.
For perpetuated cycles to change, it requires front-runners to break their cycles.
This creates pathways and a realisation in others that it is possible.
The road is not always easy, but it is fulfilling.

The reasons why people hurt each other is as varied as people.

- You may have triggered their emotional reactions, because they have judged you as their problem or blamed you for their inability to control their emotions. They might be unable to contain their emotions because you did not succumb to their control, expectations, desires, or wants.

- You may remind them of someone else, or of something they did or couldn't achieve.

- You may represent something to them that they have projected onto you, but it is not of you.

- You may represent what they yearn to be, and their jealousy is unrestrained. They have decided to defiantly oppose what you represent to protect their embedded beliefs, fears, and their worship of the illusion of control.

- You may be the victim of their belief of "I can exploit others so I will. Everyone is a commodity to be used and then discarded." A victim to their narcissism, selfishness or indifference.

- You may be the victim of their fear, which triggers them to operate with a "dog-eat-dog—get them before they get me" mentality, while they elect to disregard the truth of how you have treated them.

- You may be the victim of their desire to be soul oppressive.

- Acknowledge what your personal views are ....

....

....

Our interactions and relationships with each other are complex, but we each decide how we interact. How we interact creates energy—an action.

Our relationships with others, enables us to discover the truth of our own energy. However, discovery requires us to take self-responsibility; otherwise our relationships descend into arenas of perpetuated unconsciousness. If you have acted out the energy of your own unconsciousness, or have been triggered, unleashing cyclic patterns of behaviour, beliefs, and spoken words, you have to take ownership of that. Acknowledge your purpose, intent and consequences, and then deal with your reality truthfully. However, if another is not willing to meet you on a platform for truthfulness, you can only take responsibility for yourself. Their reactions are not all about you, and it is wise to remember they are also making a decision about how they treat others as they react.

We all lose ourselves sometimes, and our emotions can override our decision-making. This is why we give each other grace, because we know how easy it is to lose control of our own emotions. However, those who constantly refuse to take responsibility for their emotional lash-outs—even when they have calmed down—will seek to blame others, exploit the grace of others, or delight in being indifferent to the ramifications of their actions. This lack of truthfulness and indifference descends relationships into oppressive arenas, which have an impact on all involved. We can gloss-over reality believing it is a form of grace, but we won't feel the grace. Ignoring, denying or martyring ourselves to dysfunction is not giving grace. Grace is only given if the entirety of the truth is acknowledged, and when we have an acceptance of the complexities of human nature.

We should strive to provide opportunities for each other to be truthful and be someone that values truth but we cannot take responsibility for those who refuse to be accountable for themselves. Those who refuse to take self-responsibility constantly blame others in an attempt to justify their deflective judgement, over-bearing resentment, and compulsive desire to have control over another or what is perceived as truth. Their refusal to acknowledge their reality, leaves them stuck in a cyclic pattern of perpetuating their unconscious energy—unresolved emotions.

"Knowing thy self" is important because life is a shared arena that often causes us to become entwined emotionally, energetically, and physically.

Knowing what is of your energy and what is not, stems from knowing the truth of who you are and from taking responsibility for your energy.

You are responsible for you, and others are responsible for themselves. Part of self-responsibility is interacting, treating, and acknowledging others respectfully; declining to make them an arena in which to act out the unconscious energy—unresolved emotions—you refuse to be honest about.

What we choose to do with our freewill sets energy in motion,
whether we are aware of it or not.

Self-Responsibility Story

Rosalee was excited to see her old friend, Gloria. They hadn't spent time together for ages, and she was looking forward to introducing Gloria to her new boyfriend Fletcher.

Gloria was arriving on Thursday for a week, and Rosalee was busy making plans. She told Fletcher how much they loved going to the beach when they were younger, so that was on her list. She also explained that they could lose hours shopping together, and laughed as she informed him not to send a search party because they always made it home, eventually. Rosalee made a booking at her favourite restaurant, and had organised a barbeque for the weekend so they both could catch-up with old friends. Her excitement was tangible.

Fletcher hadn't officially moved in but he had stated on several occasions he couldn't bear to be separated from Rosalee, so he started coming straight from work to her place. She had never been to his home; he had implied it was too messy for company. It had been a whirlwind month, and Rosalee felt so ecstatic. She had been in a romantic bubble and was thrilled that Fletcher was about to meet her closest friend.

The barbeque was her way of introducing Fletcher to some of her friends and family. "You'll love them," Rosalee proclaimed, "They are all looking forward to meeting you."

Rosalee had taken the week off work, and Gloria arrived Thursday afternoon. They spent the afternoon catching up on each other's lives. Roselee kept singing the praise of her new beau and struggled to contain her enthusiasm.

"He is the one! My soul-mate!" she gleefully announced at the end of every statement.

Gloria giggled each time Rosalee said it, and with a big smile would reply, "I'm so happy for you!"

They started to prepare dinner and Rosalee became visibly anxious and Gloria asked, "What's wrong?"

Rosalee nervously replied, "He is always here by six o'clock, I hope he hasn't had an accident. No-one would know to contact me. I haven't met any of his friends or family. They mightn't even know I'm his girlfriend."

By seven o'clock, Rosalee was beginning to pace and was visibly distressed.

Gloria suggested ringing him.

Rosalee replied, "I have, several times, no answer, what should I do? He rings or texts me constantly throughout the day, I've been so busy that I hadn't noticed he hasn't today. What if he had an accident this morning, how will I know?"

At nine o'clock Rosalee's phone rang. She frantically answered it with, "Are you ok? I've been worried sick! Where are you?"

"Home, you didn't invite me over," replied Fletcher.

Rosalee was shocked, "Oh, I just presumed you'd be here. We talked about having dinner with Gloria here tonight."

"Why would you presume, I'm still a guest at your place. I was trying to do the right thing by you. I didn't want to disturb you and your friend. It's ok! I realise I'm not your first priority. I don't really know where I stand in this relationship," retorted Fletcher.

Rosalee began to explain how important he was in her life and she hoped they had a future together.

Fletcher replied, "Did you just ask me to move in?"

Rosalee sat for a second looking perplexed and with a gust of enthusiasm proclaimed, "No, but why not. Let's move in together."

With the same enthusiasm Fletcher announced, "I'll start bringing my stuff over tomorrow, while you two are at the beach."

Rosalee turned to Gloria, and asked, "Are you happy to go to the beach tomorrow?"

Gloria overheard the conversation and one eyebrow began to involuntary rise, as she nodded yes.

Gloria felt an uneasiness wash over her, as she watched her friend finish her phone call.

The next afternoon as they arrived back from the beach, they were confronted with a removalist truck. As they walked down the driveway, Rosalee noticed her lounge on the truck. She distressingly asked the removalist why her lounge was in there.

He replied, "I bought it off the man moving in. The rest went with the charity guys."

"What is happening?" said a bewildered Rosalee, staring blankly a Gloria.

"I'll wait here, and give you a minute to talk to Fletcher," said Gloria.

Fifteen minutes later Rosalee returned, announcing, "Everything's fine. I just have to get used to sharing my place with Fletcher and he wanted it to be our home, not just moving into mine. So, he picked the best of what we had and got rid of the rest. Isn't he wonderful, he gave it all to charity?"

"He should've asked you first. When did he organise the removalist truck? How well do you know him?" inquired Gloria.

"He is the one! My soul-mate!" snapped Rosalee, "He said others wouldn't understand our bond."

Gloria's stomach churned.

For the rest of the week, there were countless incidents of Fletcher going out of his way to disrupt Rosalee's plans. He hardly spoke to anyone at the barbeque, moodily sat in view and stared at Rosalee. She told everyone quietly that Fletcher is extremely shy and to give him time to relax.

He was late to the restaurant, constantly complaining about the food and service. He constantly belittled the waiter and Rosalee for booking such a place. Rosalee started agreeing with him and profusely apologised for her poor judgement.

He rang constantly while they were out shopping, and Rosalee eventually ushered them home citing that she felt unwell. Gloria struggled with the way Rosalee would make excuses for him. She had become irritated every time she heard Fletcher was her soul-mate, and dumb-founded by her submissive behaviour.

It was the last day of her visit and Gloria had had enough of Fletcher and feared for her friend. While they were having lunch before she caught the train, she could no longer contain her point of view.

"Rosalee, I want to be honest with you. Fletcher isn't a nice person. He is condescending and over-bearing. He is not shy, he is conniving. He is using you, controlling you! I'm worried about you."

"He told me you are jealous of our bond. We are soul-mates, and he said you'd try to ruin it for me! He said I couldn't see it because we grew-up together. You have always told me what to think!" exclaimed Rosalee as she stood up. "Find your own way to the train station."

"You have my suitcase in your car," mumbled Gloria as she followed Rosalee. "I never meant to hurt you, but it scares me what this relationship is doing to you. We have never fought or been jealous of each other. We have always been best friends. I love you and I'm telling you, I'm scared."

"Get in, I'll drop you off." Silently they headed for the train station.

As they arrived Rosalee defiantly announced, "He warned me about you! Please, don't contact me anymore, I have to embrace my new life."

"Sounds like he's speaking for you, already," Gloria said and as she got out of the car she mouthed, "I love you, friend."

Twenty years later, Rosalee now a mother of two teenage daughters, called Gloria.

"I owe you an apology. I spent eighteen years making excuses for his behaviour. I felt like a shell of a person, taught myself to not only ignore my opinion, but to not have one. I had forgotten what it was like to laugh, to relax, or how to be excited about anything. He started training me to be submissive on the first date, but I refused to acknowledge his behaviour. I wanted the fairytale. I wanted him to be my soul-mate. I gave up everything and everyone, I have no friends and I am estranged from my family.

I kept forgiving him for everything he did or said, constantly hitting the imaginary reset button. He never admitted to anything and refused to take responsibility for his behaviour. Over the years his obnoxiousness accelerated. He made me believe I was insane when I questioned him. Everything I did was wrong!

I started to believe I was the problem early on and eventually became completely indifferent towards myself. I didn't care anymore, there was nothing left of me to hurt. At the beginning of the relationship, I spent my time trying to please him. I agreed with everything he said to create harmony. I wanted to believe in him and ignored his actions. Later on, I just agreed with him in an attempt to avoid his put-downs or emotional out-bursts. I never found out how to avoid them, everything was always my fault, and for a long time I believed him." Rosalee announced hardly drawing a breath.

"Are you ok?" questioned Gloria.

"I have two beautiful daughters who fear him. A couple of years ago my eldest daughter said, *Dad, isn't a nice person. He is condescending and over-bearing. He's conniving and constantly plays mind games. He is using you and controls you! I'm worried about you. You kept making excuses for him, trying to hide who he is, but you can't.* As you know I've heard that before."

Rosalee continued as she fought back her tears.

"I left him a week later and have spent the last two years learning how to recover from my marriage. I had to take responsibility for me. I lost my ability to be honest with myself and became unwilling to acknowledge my reality. I know I was tricked and fooled, but I know that I need to get honest, so I can recover. I just wanted you to know, I'm sorry about how I treated you."

"Rosalee, when are you and your daughters coming for a visit? I live near a beach and a shopping mall," cheered Gloria.

Rosalee laughed, "Some things never change."

"Please visit, I miss my best friend, but I knew she would find her way back."

Our relationships with each other are complex and it is surprising how quickly they can change. What we believe they are and the reality of them can differ. Our wants and desires create separation between what is real and what we hope for. We use denial, avoidance and excuses to ignore reality. To uphold these, we have to forgo valuing truth, which chips away at our willingness to take self-responsibility and accountability for the decisions we make.

Rosalee is the victim of an abusive relationship and did not intentionally lack self-responsibility. She shifted her mind-set because she wanted to be loved by the man she thought Fletcher was, and ignored the red flags. She took on responsibility for keeping him content—an impossible task—and unwittingly became trapped in his web of deceit. She became blinded by her desire for a soul-mate, and he became her priority, while devaluing her own emotional and spiritual wellbeing. This happened so quickly for her that she didn't realise what was truly occurring.

She originally believed in her partner and wanted to continue to do so, even when there was undeniable evidence that he was not who she wanted him to be. He knew exactly how to make her doubt herself. He told her what she wanted to hear, and set himself up to be the prize she was looking for—the prince in her fairytale. He also knew how to undermine and destroy her other relationships—isolating her.

Rosalee was blinded by the false promises and the original excitement. She believed they could return to those days, and clung to this desire. Her daughter's honesty became the catalyst for accepting her reality. This acceptance set the wheels in motion for change. She could no-longer ignore reality, she had no more excuses left, and decided to take responsibility for herself. This is confronting, but with each step she took the veils of denial fell and her inner-strength came to the forefront.

Rosalee realised she had martyred herself to his dysfunction and had become emotionally, energetically, and physically entwined with it. Part of her recovery process is discovering who she is—Knowing thy self. Her past has a lot to teach her.

As she recognises her cyclic patterns of behaviour, beliefs, and internal dialogue, she'll heal the wounds.

As she acknowledges her original intent to be in a loving relationship and how it differed from his, which was to possess and demoralise her, she'll stop blaming herself.

When our actions or the actions of others have caused pain and dispirited us, it is difficult to come to terms with the motives fuelling these hurtful actions. Recovering from painful experiences requires us to remove all false filters and desired illusions that shield us from acknowledging the truth.

As Rosalee accepts the reasons behind Fletcher's behaviour, and acknowledges it had nothing to do with who she is, she'll no longer allow him or her past to define her worth.

As she comes to terms with the motives behind her decisions, she'll embrace the value of truthfulness, and develop an honest relationship with herself.

The consequences have played out, and will possibly reverberate throughout her life. However, now she has an opportunity to deal with her reality truthfully and accept the journey of self-discovery is ongoing.

Self-responsibility enables us to honestly explore reality.
Accepting reality is how we learn, grow and heal.

SECTION 4

Feed your soul by reflecting on what you are reading.
Spiritual and emotional growth requires nurturing,
extract the nutrients from your insight and awareness
triggered by your resonance with the information in the books.

Chapters 10–14 are peppered with optional questions. Write down your answer to the questions, include thoughts, and feelings triggered by these questions. Without reviewing what you have written, redo the questions at a later date—upon completion of reading each chapter, perhaps after you have finished the entire section or two weeks after you put the book down. Then compare your answers. This often highlights what you internally knew or have learnt, enabling you to acknowledge your awareness growth and soul maturity.

Choose the questions you are interested in and leave the rest. You may do the others another time. This is a trust-how-you-feel exercise. This process is used in different formats throughout all the books in the Insight and Awareness Anthology. Your insight and awareness matters, and it helps to have a process for acknowledging it.

The dotted lines are reminders to acknowledge and explore your own thoughts, awareness, and feelings.

I recommend using a separate journal to write your answers, so you can use this questionnaire numerous times without being influenced by what you have previously written.

For your convenience,
free downloadable PDF questionnaires are available at
lorrainenilon.com.au/ytsv

CHAPTER TEN
When Did Truth Become the Enemy?

1. When did we allow the fear of expressing our souls—authenticity, to deter us from exploring truth?

....

....

2. When did we start denying our unconditional love for the truth of our origins?

....

....

3. When did we entrust our soul journey to our soul immaturity?

....

....

4. Why do we disassociate from the truth we feel? Identify the feelings you withdraw from and struggle to acknowledge.

....

....

5. Why are we complacent about our internal and external reality?

....

....

6. Why do we separate from our awareness of our soul's consciousness?

....

....

7. Why do we desperately seek validation from those who do not want to feel truth and are willing to deny the essence of their own soul?

....

....

8. Why do we camouflage the true essences of our souls?

....

....

9. Why are images and illusions more enticing than truth?

....

....

10. Why do we ignore our awareness and insightfulness?

....

....

11. Why do we desire to control truth?

....

....

These are big questions to ask! We often lie to ourselves about the reality of who we are to avoid truthfully answering these types of questions.

O ur separation from our awareness of our soul and our disassociation from feeling truth are a result of our denial of the significance of who we are. We are unique souls with an opportunity to evolve to feel the exquisiteness of who we are.

When we deny ourselves an opportunity to explore our soul truth, we start believing our unresolved emotions, damaging self-beliefs, and negative thoughts are true. However, they are the result of our impaired self-awareness and this leads to perceiving truth as an enemy, before we have comprehended the value of truth. Instead of rejecting unresolved emotions, damaging self-beliefs, and negative thoughts, we can use our recognition of them to direct us to meaningful self-explorations. We need to acknowledge what requires resolution, before we can honestly resolve them.

We often attempt to fool ourselves into believing we can control the energy of our soul's unconsciousness—our unresolved emotions—and secure an image of ourselves, but this is a choice to abandon the exploration of who we are. When we abandon the willingness to explore the truth of ourselves, both our conscious and unconscious energy, we resist our awareness of truth. Our struggle against self-acceptance leaves us opposing the reality of being a soul and will even cause us to doubt our souls' existence. This stems from the desire to deny responsibility for what we have stored in our unconsciousness.

We can choose to abandon the exploration of truth because we fear being judged, ridicule or ostracised. This leads to a hidden belief that an awareness of truth inhibits our ability to control ourselves within our reality; we fear truth will disrupt our ability to control.

12. What is it that we want to control that is more important to us than the truth of our souls? *Our image is one answer. What is another answer?*

....

....

We fear being judged, ridiculed or ostracised because we have denied the significance of who we naturally are. This causes us to deny our opportunity to awaken to the consciousness of our souls. We deny how we give the fear of judgement power over the way we feel about ourselves.

> *When you do not challenge the intent of others' judgements*
> *or the motives behind your own judgement, you*
> *become trapped by your fear of judgement.*

Our fear of judgement has us seeking validation for our limited perception of ourselves and often has us ostracising ourselves from our own awareness of truth.

We ridicule ourselves for not feeling alive, joyful, and authentic; and then we create images, illusions and controlled identities to keep ourselves in the emotional limbo that sustains our evolutionary idle. Our evolutionary idle exposes our decision to fight the presence of truth with our desire for control and soul-oppressive energy.

Our evolutionary idle means we remain stuck reverberating with unconscious energy while opposing the free-flowing frequency of our consciousness. Our evolutionary idle lets us exist in systems designed to oppress us, and they are recognisable by the way they feed the belief of "not being good enough". It is an idle that doesn't let us live to our full potential. Our potential expands from the essences of our souls and contracts when they are devalued.

Our evolutionary idle sustains constructed life plans based on wants, while we avoid our present moment and deny the ramifications of our denial.

You may say you want the freedom to resolve and evolve your evolutionary idle, and strongly believe you want to experience being beyond your own self-manipulation and the exploitation of others.

However, if you seek approval and validation from others about your value, worth, and significance or cultivate the desire to control your consciousness, you have rejected your opportunity for freedom.
You are saying one thing while doing another.

Sometimes we do not realise we are stuck in an evolutionary idle, because we are busy distracting ourselves with things that sustain our resistance to truth, denial of reality, and avoidance of self-responsibility.

We use our wants to manipulate ourselves to remain trapped by our own evolutionary idle, because we have chosen to constantly pit our desire for control against the value of truth. We are competing against truth to protect the energy of our soul's unconsciousness and forsake the consciousness of our souls to do so.

13. Why do we want to control truth and our own consciousness?
Is it because we find it hard to accept the truth of ourselves and our actions?

....

....

14. Why do we desperately seek approval for our performance of unconscious energy, when at the core of our being we are of conscious energy?

....

....

When we allow ourselves to be victimised by our self-opposing judgement, we wallow in the ramifications of abandoning our awareness of truth. One of the ramifications is the belief of not being good enough. Another is the anxiety of fearing we can't control ourselves, truth, others, or our life experiences. We are often oblivious to the reality that our abandonment of truth stems from the desire to secure an illusion of control.

You have experienced abandoning truth, if you have caught yourself:

- Lying to yourself.
- Operating in denial.
- Resisting admission of your own awareness.
- Avoiding taking responsibility for your own behaviour, beliefs, and the words you speak.

We can become fearful of our desire for control, because we know we are worshipping control and devaluing truth. We recognise the fear of feeling powerless. We feel the building tension and the emotional explosion or implosion that follows. We also know we will emotionally react to the internal tension we create from our opposition to truth.

We instinctively know the internal tension is an indication we are not being our authentic selves—we are not in the flow of consciousness. Even though we often cannot articulate this, there is an internal warning signal—an undercurrent of fear that we are missing the purpose and meaning of life. Our fear exposes an internal knowing that we are refusing to take responsibility for the orchestration of our own soul oppression.

Soul oppression is the active force you generate from the energies stored in your soul's unconsciousness, which you use to emotionally, energetically and physically oppress your awareness of your truth.

Your soul truth is the reality of both your conscious and unconscious energy.

We are fearful of acknowledging our separation from our awareness of truth and how capable we are of betraying our soul's consciousness. We are unsure as to why we oppress our awareness of being a soul, but it is a result of our freewill.

Throughout history, we have victimised each other in our pursuit of control. We have wanted ownership over what is considered the truth of our origins. We've done this while denying the price it costs our souls. Our individual and collective pursuit of control over truth has left us with a legacy of unconscious energy and systems that were created to sustain separation from our awareness of truth. These systems perpetuate the energy we carry within our soul's unconsciousness. This is our collective karma. Karma is the law of cause and effect—the consequences of our decisions and actions.

We have obscured our awareness of the presence of truth—the flow of consciousness within all that exists—and declared we are innocent of our own deceptive manipulation which has caused us to devalue our relationship with truth.

Spirituality is an expedition to develop a meaningful relationship with truth.

15. What are we desperately trying to prove when we deny the truth we feel and the evidence of the consequences of our denial?

....

....

16. Are we trying to prove to ourselves that we have control over reality, or that we can control ourselves to be indifferent to reality? What has been the cause and effect of our pursuit of control?

....

....

17. What are we trying to prove when we deliberately oppose our own awareness of truth?

....

....

18. In what ways do we avoid unconditional love and the reality of being souls with evolutionary potential?

....

....

19. Do we deny that we independently choose how we feel about ourselves and what we are doing? How does our denial affect our interactions with each other?

....

....

20. Why do we deny ourselves opportunities to explore our codependency on the cyclic patterns of our soul oppression? Why are we willing to protect our codependency on the lies we tell ourselves?

....

....

21. Why do we deny responsibility for ourselves, and what does this create?

....

....

22. Our acknowledgement of our own truth opens the door to our journey to freedom. What do we need freedom from?

....

....

23. Are we forcing ourselves to be disassociated from feeling our own soul truth and the reality of our origins? How do we sustain this disassociation?

....

....

When we deny our individuality and perceive ourselves as a collective, we lose the individuality of our spiritualism. We define ourselves by how we categorize our differences, such as religion, race, gender, prejudices, sexual orientations, location, finances, or .... Instead of identifying ourselves as individuals within a collective, we take the beliefs, behaviours, and judgements of the collective to define an identity. We have used our collective identities to create division and the desire to conquer each other, denying we are individuals within the collective of humanity.

We are individuals within the collective of humanity.
Humanity is the collective of souls within a physical body,
experiencing life as creators.

We create energy and experiences that have
a cause and effect known as
karma.

Our individuality is an expression of the purity of our soul's frequency, and we oppose this to preserve the herd mentality that sustains our immaturity.

We reverberate with the energy within the collectives we use to create identities, allowing our prejudices and judgements to form belief systems. Denial of our humanity creates oppressive soul energy, because we have fundamentally forsaken the flow of consciousness within humanity. Once forsaken, separation from our internal knowing and awareness of our souls starts a chain reaction that creates further separation from truth. When we abandon our awareness of the individuality of our souls, we become reverberations of unconscious energy within the collectives we use as identities. Harmony becomes devalued and the seven deadly sins take hold of our attention and intentions.

Our differences illustrate the diversity of soul experiences,
but do not explain the truth of our souls.

We attempt to oppress the core of our being with our unconscious energy, seeking to control the divinity of our soul. However, the divinity of our soul is naturally free-flowing consciousness, and we can only control ourselves to deny awareness. We swamp our awareness with soul-oppressive energy to deny the divinity of ourselves. When we individually choose to acknowledge the truth of how we have become entrapped by our own soul-oppressive energy, beliefs, and behaviours, we become an opportunity for consciousness to expand on earth.

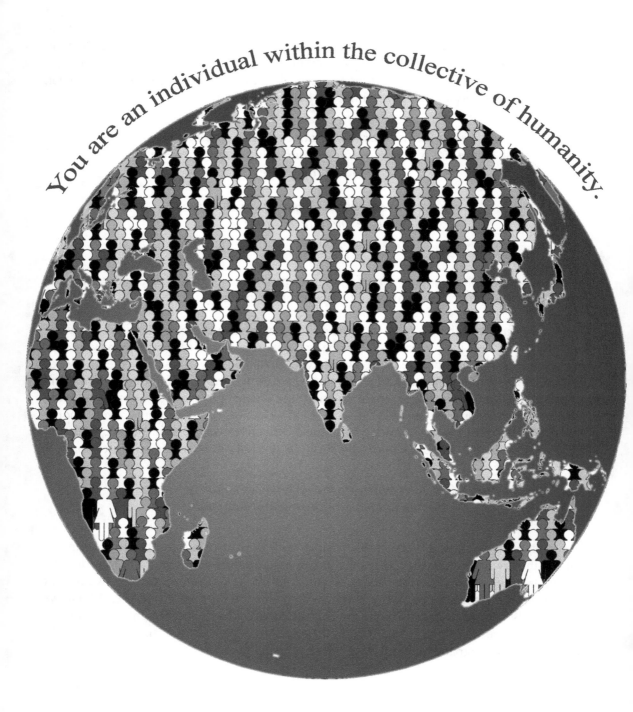

You are an individual within the collective of humanity.

Think of it this way:

We surrounded our consciousness with unconscious energy, similar to an island surrounded by a polluted ocean. We believe we are part of the polluted ocean and ignore the island. We have struggled to adapt and exist in the pollution. We have exerted a lot of time and effort trying to control the pollution to be what we want it to be. We have denied the reality that we created the polluted ocean, because we rejected the comforts of the island.

We generate waves of oppressive energy that swamp the island, trying to make it uninhabitable and unrecognisable; in an attempt to justify our rejection of its comfort, value and majesticness. The island is never damaged and offers us an opportunity to rejuvenate ourselves, if we are prepared to leave the polluted ocean.

The island is stronger than the ocean, but we ignore this fact and continue to pollute the ocean we created. As the vastness of the polluted ocean expands, our awareness of the island diminishes, but it is still there, awaiting our return, holding to the truth of our origins.

To be part of the expansion of consciousness, we need to turn to the core essences of our souls, such as compassion and grace. This only occurs when we decide to explore beyond our denial, and are no longer willing to ignore the significance of our soul's consciousness. From here we can acknowledge the reality of our own creation of unconsciousness and purposely align with the voyage of converting unconsciousness into the expansion of consciousness.

As we unify with the core essences of our soul,
we realise truth is not the enemy.
The enemy is our denial.

When we enslaved ourselves to the struggle of oppressing our own individuality, conformed to our desire for control, tolerated being indifferent to truth, and operated from the seven deadly sins, we became reverberations of unconscious energy.

Our unconscious energy reverberates with the energetic collectives of the mass energy of mankind, which correlates with the energy of our own soul's unconsciousness. We are part of the creation and sustainability of the collective unconsciousness of mankind. This becomes a mutual exchange of energy. We feed the collective with energy, and that energy is attracted to us because it is vibrating within our system.

If you have been to a sporting event or concert, and the crowd was cheering and in high spirits, and you found yourself aligning with that energy—cheering—you have reacted to mass energy. If you've been in a room full of judgemental people and realised you started to be judgmental, you reacted to that energy. But here is the catch, if you didn't have judgement in you, you couldn't be triggered. If you didn't want to have a good time at the sporting event or concert, you wouldn't have joined in. Sometimes we surprise ourselves with the energy that affects us, and it may suggest an exploration is required to understand why.

The denial of our contribution to the collective unconsciousness and our own soul's unconsciousness has resulted in the repetition of our soul-denial history. History repeats if not learnt from, and when the truth is oppressed. This has us individually and collectively anchored to our indifference to the truth of our souls.

We have wanted control over the separation from our awareness of our souls and disassociation from feeling truth—to deny responsibility for our creation of unconscious energy. However, our control is only an illusion. We internally know truth is never separated from truth, and truth is never disassociated from reality. Regardless of the proficiency of our control, we rely on an illusion to fool ourselves about being separated from truth. Truth is always present, and the truth of whatever we do is creating a cause and effect, which is reality.

No matter how separated or disassociated from our awareness, truth is always the fundamental energy. Our separation and disassociation are illusions of our control and a result of our loss of awareness of our own reality.

Mankind's Energetic Collectives

Energetic mankind collective of rage

Energetic mankind collective of elitism

Energetic mankind collective of superiority

Energetic mankind collective of guilt

Energetic mankind collective of shame

Energetic mankind collective of humiliation

Energetic mankind collective of spiritual Illusion

Energetic mankind collective of envy

Energetic mankind collective of resentment

superiority

elitism

rage

guilt

shame

humiliation

spiritual illusion

envy

resentment

Soul Denial

Truth is either accepted or denied. We cannot manipulate, control, or banish the presence of truth. We only do this to our own awareness of truth and maybe others' awareness of truth. Regardless of our skill to be deceptive, truth will always be there—sometimes hidden, completely ignored, but never ineffectual.

We can create an illusion to manipulate ourselves and others into denying opportunities to be aware of truth and reality, but truth will always be present. Our interaction with truth has a cause and effect that eventually our denial cannot surpass.

- We attempt to manipulate each other's awareness of truth, but truth is still there when we are willing to honestly look and trust what we feel.

- We can hide from our awareness of truth by focusing on the lies that obscure it. However, truth is still there, it is the foundation—the reality, that deception is built on.

- We can attempt to control the perception of truth, but the truth of any reality is still there.

- We can banish our awareness of truth, when we decide truth is of no value to what we want, but truth is still there.

- We become horrified by what we do to truth and the lengths to which we will go to separate from our awareness of truth, but truth is always there.

- When our collective or individual manipulation of truth and illusions of control come to light, we feel shame because we devalued the importance of truth.

Truth instinctively matters to us.

When our wants and desires overshadow the significance of truth, we align with the notion that truth is an enemy to our desire for control. This notion has allowed our manipulation of our awareness of truth to hurt our relationship with who we naturally are. Truth is our divine essence, which we have at times deceptively denied so we could create an illusion of control.

24. How long do we want to continue, to devalue truth, and what is the purpose of this?

....

....

Our resolution and evolution opportunities are within the junctures, where we recognise our freedom of choice to distinguish the difference between our soul's consciousness and our soul's unconsciousness. We choose the energy we are of and contribute to our life experiences. Recognising we have a choice awakens our awareness of our souls.

Our denial of our own unconscious energy enables us to turn life into an arena for all the ways we try to prove our unconscious energy is superior to truth. We apply a lot of effort into protecting our denial and the unconscious energy we deny. We deceptively and defiantly dominate our life experience with our desire to control life to reaffirm the strength of our unconsciousness. We have inverted the purpose of life, which is to awaken to the strength of our consciousness. This leaves us wanting our control energy to be our own mini god without truly understanding the concept of being a creator with freewill. *Creator of energy, experiences, and karma.*

We create and then deny the energy we inflict upon others and ourselves, yet we intensely acknowledge the unconscious energy inflicted upon us and how we feel. Our desire to control or to have the world revolve around our wants and desires generates a wide variety of unconscious energy, especially if we refuse to acknowledge the value of truth.

Indifference, resentment, manipulation, jealousy and the seven deadly sins stem from the devaluation of truth.

25. What unconscious energies would you like to add to the list?

   Devaluation of truth creates ....

We remember how it felt to be humiliated, exploited, classed as insignificant, or abused in any way.

26. What would you like to add to the list?

   We remember how it felt to be ....

It's easy to dwell on how another treated us, but how often do we contemplate how our actions have affected others? It's difficult to be an objective observer of our own behaviour because we are too busy trying to justify it. Acknowledging our behaviour should never be an invitation to beat ourselves up. We need to take time for reflection that lets us acknowledge the truth of our purpose, original intent, and consequences so we can learn from our experiences.

When you feel guilt—believe or know you have done something wrong, harmful, or exploitive—it is an indication you have a conscience or empathy. If you use this to develop shame—the belief that there is something wrong with who you are—it is easy to get caught in the cyclic pattern of self-indulgent oppression. Shame can motivate you to hide from acknowledging the truth of your actions. This means you will not confront your reality or do what you can to make amends. You will wallow in the oppression, refusing to learn from or examine the potential within the experience.

What we feel we are a victim to is often at the forefront. It generates pain that festers within and needs to be respectfully addressed. It's difficult to acknowledge what this pain caused us to do to others. I've found discussing how we have intentionally or unintentionally victimised another is fraught with danger. I have often witnessed an implosion of guilt that is then followed with how they are victim to their own emotions, including guilt. There are varying reactions to being offended even when we know it is true. This is not to judge them, but how do we evolve if we refuse to look at the truth of everything that has a cause and effect on our lives?

Confronting ourselves is difficult, and it takes a brave soul to acknowledge and grow from all our experiences.

27. Identify the last unconscious energy—negative emotions—you inflicted on another.

....

....

    a) How did you make them feel because you couldn't restrain your unconscious energy?

....

....

    b) Identify the purpose—the reason why, you did what you did.

....

....

    c) Identify the intent—emotions, you wanted to put in motion.

....

....

    d) Identify the consequences—the wake of your actions.

....

....

Truth is not the enemy; it is our liberator.
Empathy is a balancer and a key element to our ability to evolve.

Empathy is the ability to identify and feel another's emotions and feelings. It is the willingness to try to understand their experiences by contemplating what it would be like if it was our experience. This can become out of balance when we are in another's emotions and living them as if they were our own. When we struggle to identify what our emotions are or what we have adopted from another, we become out of balance with ourselves. Empathy requires balance to be of value; otherwise, it becomes an enmeshment and a loss of independence. For some, it's difficult to hold to the truth of their energy, and they are extremely impacted by the energies of others.

If you don't understand energy, being a sensitive empathic can be emotionally, mentally, and physically draining. It also creates a mammoth amount of self-doubt, constantly trying to work out what is occurring or has occurred. The confusion becomes something that triggers an emotional implosion, followed by anxiety. Understanding and recognising your own energy is imperative to comprehending the energy exchange experienced.

Empathy is important because it exposes the truth of both conscious and unconscious energy. Empathising with another is a way of recognising their natural significance. When we acknowledge the significance of others, it assists us in becoming more mindful of our own behaviour, and this is a stepping-stone to evolution.

Empathy stems from recognising the significance of our souls.

Chapter Eleven
When Did Humanity Become the Enemy?

We are part of divinity and humanity. When we forget the truth of our souls and operate from the energy stored in our soul's unconsciousness, one of the ramifications is we forget the reality of the bigger picture. This can cause us to devalue our humanity. When we accept we are souls in a physical body, and resolve the energy of our unconsciousness, we enhance the humanity of the world. Understanding that we contribute to the humanity of the world, adds value to our evolutionary process.

- *Humanity* refers to us as a collective when we operate from or recognise, we are souls in a physical body. We are of our humanity when we collectively resonate with the truth within our souls. It stems from acknowledging our equality and of being from a united origin. Humanity is felt when we collectively operate from our soul's consciousness and emanate our core essences. We are of humanity when we acknowledge that we are souls who care about each other.

- *Mankind* refers to us as a collective when we forsake or deny we are souls in a physical body. We are of mankind when we collectively resist, deny, or avoid truth. It stems from a rejection of equality and arrogantly ignores that we are from a united origin. We are of mankind energy when we lose awareness of our humanity and devalue our souls. Mankind energy is felt when we collectively operate from our soul's unconsciousness and oppose the core essences of our souls.

Life is an evolutionary journey, an arena for us to be creators with freewill and an opportunity to freely unify with consciousness—divinity—that flows with our souls.

We get lost trying to control the world to accommodate our unconsciousness and forget who we naturally are. This dulls our awareness, and we reject our insight. Awakening to the reality of our soul truth, both consciousness and unconsciousness, requires us to be truthful and explorative. Both are required to expand our awareness.

We cannot control ourselves to be insightful, because the desire for control impedes awareness. Insightfulness reflects our respect for truth and humanity. It means we no longer desire to fight or compete against truth—we yearn to understand truth. Insightfulness is born of understanding.

We do not have to be in control of our experience or end up with the results we want, to operate from the desire for control. Projecting an image of ourselves, denying reality, or lying to ourselves, exerts control energy, all of which perpetuates the energy of our soul's unconsciousness. This in turn fuels the collective unconsciousness—the energetic mass energy of mankind.

- Our soul's consciousness is the mature aspect of us that instinctively accepts and trusts in the value of truth, because it has never abandoned being of truth.

- Our soul's unconsciousness is the immature aspect of us we created, which causes us to compulsively deny and reject the value of truth.

- We are the interface of both our consciousness and unconsciousness.

- Our soul's consciousness is the mature aspect of who we are and the part of us that is willing and seeks to resolve our unconsciousness to evolve beyond the enclave created by our soul oppression.

- Our soul's consciousness is the mature aspect of who we are that is the voice of our internal knowing, intuition, and insightfulness. It is the part of us that acknowledges the reality of our life experiences.

- Our soul consciousness' intention—our original intention for life—is to resolve the unconscious energy we've created and carry in the unconsciousness of our soul, so we can freely resonate with truth and be unified with the true essence of the divinity of our soul.

- Our soul's consciousness' intention—our original intention for life—is to be unified with the unconditional love within our souls and within our origins—*True Source Divine Origin Consciousness*.

We have never been abandoned by our origins of truth—*True Source Divine Origin Consciousness*. Our freewill—to be our own creators—has always been respected by our origins of truth. What we created that cannot reside in consciousness— unconscious energy—is our own responsibility. It is up to us when we take responsibility for our creations, and *True Source Divine Origin Consciousness* awaits our return to the expansion of consciousness—its original intention for life.

True Source Divine Origin Consciousness—our origins—knows the truth of our souls and the unique frequency of our essence. Each of us is an independent soul who is part of the evolution of collective consciousness. We are living as a soul in a physical body to create opportunities to awaken to the reality that our soul is an eternal element, connected to our origins. *You are of True Source Divine Origin Consciousness, and have the potential to evolve.* All our experiences expose the symphony of truth and create opportunities for us to unify with the truth of being a soul.

Mankind's Energetic Collectives

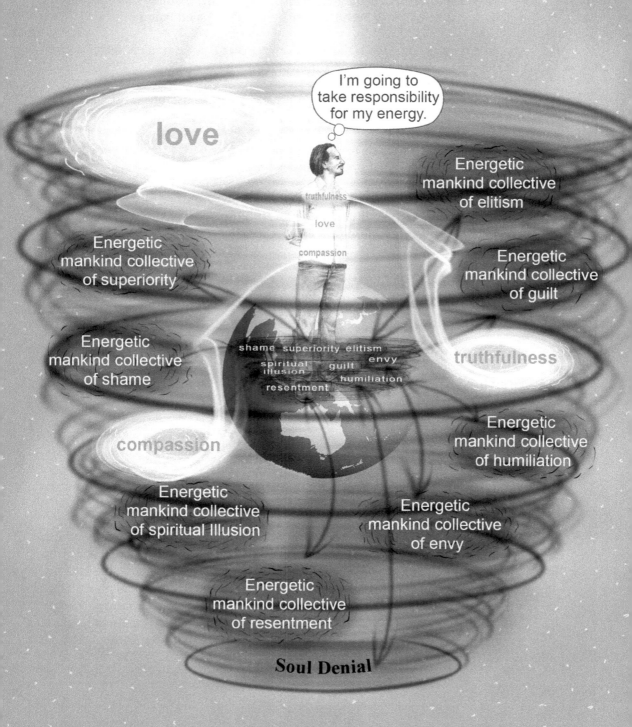

We have the freedom to choose between the following:

- Controlling ourselves to be stagnant in our unconscious energy—unresolved emotions—with apathy towards the truth of our soul's consciousness. This causes us to become anti-our own soul truth and stuck in an evolutionary idle, because we are unwilling to be truthful with ourselves.

Or

- We accept the reality of all the energy we are experiencing and acknowledge the truth within the dynamics of our life, while trusting we are an element of our origins of truth—*True Source Divine Origin Consciousness*. Accepting the option to be truthful about ourselves—what we feel and how we react and respond to our present moment.

When we camouflage that we have choices, and deny the motive behind our decisions, we reject our ability to feel truth. We corrupt ourselves with our fear of acknowledging the truth of our own soul-oppressive energy, behaviours, thoughts, and words. We can become fraudulent with our opportunities to live aware and awakened to our own natural significance.

This lifetime is temporary,
but our soul is not.

On the scale of Earth's timeline, each life we have had is minuscule, which does not mean it is insignificant, just that it is a speck of time in regard to the immensity of our souls. However, the significance of our soul's evolution is immeasurable.

We are souls participating in the evolution of *True Source Divine Origin Consciousness*' resolution of its' unconscious energy. Our soul's unconsciousness is our portion of the unconscious energy of *True Source Divine Origin Consciousness*. The collective unconsciousness—the energetic mass energy of mankind—we have all contributed to, is the energy *True Source Divine Origin Consciousness* endeavours to resolve and evolve. Each of us are responsible for our contribution to the collective unconsciousness, and as each brave soul resolves and evolves their portion, they become participants in the evolution of *True Source Divine Origin Consciousness*.

When we deny the significance of our souls, we deny the significance of *True Source Divine Origin Consciousness*' evolution. Our denial creates emotional, energetic, and physical anarchy within ourselves, anaesthetising our awareness of our soul's consciousness and truth, often because we fear the significance of who we are or because the illusion of control has become all that we hold sacred.

Our soul's consciousness is directly connected to the purity of our origins of truth—*True Source Divine Origin Consciousness*. We are of truth. When we fear the purity of truth, we anesthetise our awareness of our soul's consciousness and attempt to control ourselves to the illusion of being separated from the process of *True Source Divine Origin Consciousness'* evolution. We attempt to allow our desire for control to reign supreme while losing awareness of our original intent for life as an evolutionary journey.

Our expectation of life becomes about securing an illusion of control, and we fasten to the illusions we use to shield ourselves from our internal and external reality. These illusions are secured by the narrative we tell ourselves. This causes us to remain lost, yet we believe we are in control.

We inhibit ourselves from acknowledging the bigger picture of our significance and are willing to dumb ourselves down to be the perpetuator of unconsciousness. We hide from the magnitude and significance of our own and *True Source Divine Origin Consciousness'* evolution, because we fear losing the ability to create and sustain illusions.

We use our unconscious energy—unresolved emotions—to dominate our perception of reality and focus our attention on what we believe is, or could possibly interfere with, our control. This leads to us fighting our own awareness of truth. This causes us to discount the importance of acknowledging our humanity. We forget we were born to share the world with others and to be nurturers—supporters of the evolutionary potential of humanity.

We choose what we fight and how we fight against it. We often don't even ask what we are fighting.

CHAPTER TWELVE
When Did Awareness Become the Enemy?

We will fight our awareness of our emotional, energetic, and physical reality, with our denial, resentment, and indifference, seeking to have ownership of how reality should be, to appease our own desire for control. This causes us to reject opportunities within our reality, dogmatically expecting to create what we want and believe we desire, without actually comprehending what we are doing to our souls.

When we worship our own wants and desires with little regard for truth, we internally and externally struggle if we cannot appease our desire for control or sustain our illusion of having control. When our control fails to deliver what we want, we become disheartened and disillusioned with life. It is only a true failure if we are unable to observe the truth of what has occurred. When we acknowledge the truth of ourselves and the energy contributing to what we have considered failure, we acknowledge an opportunity to learn from what we have assessed as failure or an error in judgement.

Our resolution occurs through the awareness of truth. We use our desire for control to conceal this from ourselves, which leaves us fearful of being unable to sustain an illusion of control. Resolve the desire for control, and an illusion of control is no longer wanted. Acknowledge our awareness, and control becomes recognisable. If we deny our awareness, we struggle to recognise the reality of our control, wants, and desires. We just react unconsciously to them.

It is our difficulty to acknowledge
the truth of ourselves that inhibits our evolutionary process.
Our resistance to, and avoidance of truth steers us to perceive
any truth that does not align with our wants and desires as the enemy.

When we allow ourselves to be manipulated by our desire for control or desperately want to observe the effect our control has over others' awareness of truth, we become an opponent against our own evolution. This causes us to pit the energy of our soul's unconsciousness against the energy of our soul's consciousness. We perceive ourselves as a dichotomy of two separated energies and in an arena for a contrived competition; competing against our awareness of truth and our own flow of consciousness. This creates an evolutionary idle.

We have the freedom and can choose to remain in an idle. It is through our decision to be truthful about ourselves that we will convert the competition into a learning opportunity; otherwise, this competition we have orchestrated becomes an arena to act out our own soul oppression—to be creators of unconsciousness.

When we betray our own awareness of our souls, we abandon our authenticity. We are the perpetuator of our soul oppression. This causes our indifference towards ourselves to become fuel for our framework of soul oppression. Our framework of soul oppression is sequenced patterns of emotional reactions that incite unconscious behaviour, negative thoughts, and beliefs that stem from the cause and effect of our indifference towards ourselves, others, and reality.

For more information on the framework of soul oppression, see Overview of Your Energetic System

28. Identify a sequenced pattern of emotional reactions that leaves you feeling oppressed.

    a) First I ....

        Then I ....

        These trigger ....

    b) Identify some of the thoughts that fuel the emotional ricochet.

        ....

        ....

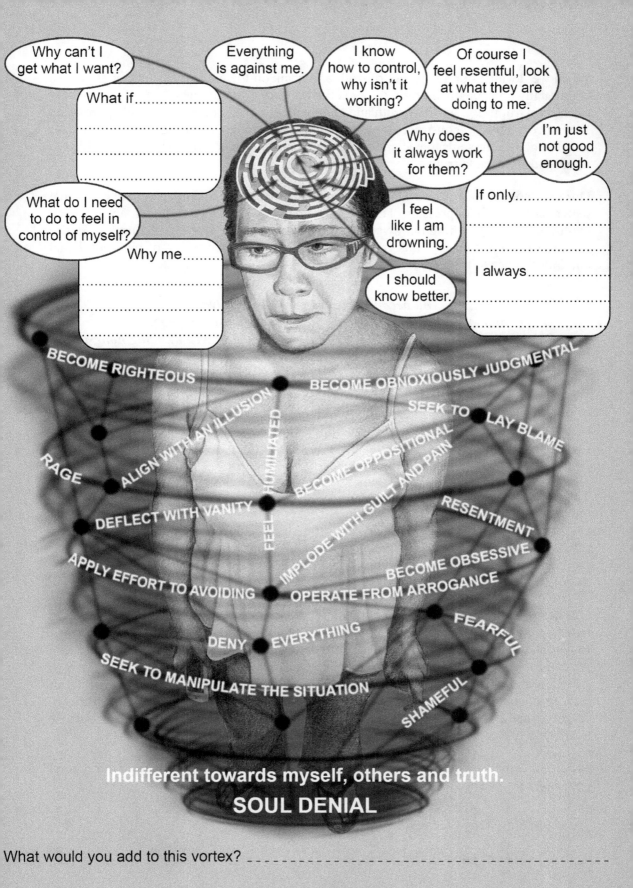

What would you add to this vortex? _____
_____
_____

When we devalue our awareness of truth and abandon the authenticity of our souls, we emotionally and negatively react to our self-discovery opportunities. Instead of choosing to respond truthfully, we deny truth and align with our cyclic patterns of soul oppression. We unconsciously construct the sequenced emotional reactions and allow our indifference to our souls to become an interceptor of our freedom. Our denial shackles us to our indifference to truth.

Our resistance to and avoidance of being truthful enables us to perpetuate the emotional patterns of our soul oppression. This means we are choosing to remain stagnant and in an evolutionary idle, fighting our awareness of reality with our illusion of control or desire for control. Unfortunately, this is how we orchestrate the protection of our soul denial and indifference to truth.

You become what you will not resolve,
and lose awareness of the truth of your soul in that process.
Spirituality is reconnection to your soul, which is achieved by being honest
about your interaction with yourself, others, life and truth.

We become what we will not resolve, existing within our unresolved emotions because of our denial of our unresolved emotions. Our denial causes us to arrogantly align with the slyness of our indifference to truth, which enables us to use our denial to empower our illusion of control. This fuels the desire to be superior to all we encounter, which can be performed in a myriad of ways.

The suppression of our emotions is born of our illusion of control, because we believe our suppression rids us of what we do not want to be honest about; therefore we are controlled. Our suppressed emotions become an undercurrent within us that we may refuse to acknowledge, but regularly act out. We have controlled our denial of our emotions and rejected our awareness, but we haven't controlled the emotion to be dormant.

Our desire to secure an image of ourselves that hides our emotions, and our illusion of having control over reality causes us to overlook the truth of our behaviour. This leads us to lose awareness of the entirety of our soul experience and to fixate on what we believe we can control or on controlling how we are perceived by others. We stagnate in our own denial, remain dumbed down and unconscious to the truth of our souls, reality, and our own resonance with truth. When we are unconscious to our resonance with truth, we forget we are of divinity—*True Source Divine Origin Consciousness*. This means we lose awareness of our souls' origins.

When we deny the significance of our uniqueness and the meaningfulness of our natural core essences, we become:

- Submissive to our fears.

- Echoes of our soul-denial history.

- Tolerant of our indifference to truth.

- Compliant to the familiarity of our soul oppression.

- Subservient to the protection of the energy of our soul's unconsciousness.

- Enslaved to our desire for control and obsessed with securing an illusion of control.

- Acknowledge what your personal views are ....

....

These cause us to disassociate from feeling our connection to ourselves and our origins of truth. We disassociate from feeling and align with what we believe secures an illusion of control, retrograding our soul's evolution by adhering to the unconsciousness of our soul. Our unresolved emotions become what are prominent, as we willingly reiterate our soul-denial history. This can cause us to be transfixed on ruminating about how to get our control to work or about how disappointed we are because our control has already failed. We also ruminate about justifying the emotions we realise we can't suppress or deny.

We oppose our awareness of our soul truth,
both our consciousness and unconsciousness,
because we have decided it does not suit what we want to believe.

When we deny the trustworthiness of our soul's consciousness and reject our awareness of *True Source Divine Origin Consciousness'* existence, we allow our distrust to cloud our perception of reality. We can dictate what our divinity is and wants from us, in an attempt to justify our beliefs. This often causes us to become obsessed with proving we are righteous in our judgement and entitled to inflict our demands for control on those who do not succumb to our expectations.

We inflict our demands for control onto each other in many different ways, all of which leave us with the feeling of being oppressed and exploited. There is a difference between asking someone to align with what we believe is required or would like to occur, to demanding control over them.

Some demand control by:

- Inciting fear in another.

- Being manipulative to get what they want.

- Being sly—operating with dishonest intent.

- Sulking in despair until another is coerced into appeasing them.

- Being indifferent, disregarding everything except their own demands.

- Being intimidating as they dogmatically pursue the actualisation of their demands.

- Being slothful, waiting for another to take responsibility for what they want to occur.

- Acknowledge what your personal views are ....

  ....

  ....

Once the desire for control has been established and demands made, we can become obsessed with wanting to witness the cause and effect of our control. This desire fuels narcissism, selfishness, indifference, resentment, and many more unconscious energies.

Wanting to witness our control affecting others, our reality, and how truth is perceived has plagued mankind. It has left us pitting our control, desires, and wants against our own awareness of truth. Instead of unifying with truth, truth becomes the enemy of our desires. We often align with deception hoping it will provide us with what we believe we want, willing to devalue truth because it is convenient to our wants and desires. We'll ride the deception and only acknowledge truth if there is no other alternative. We rely on ours and others' denial to shield us from the truth of our actions. We can delight in getting away with deception and then use a corrupted narrative to justify our actions and beliefs.

When we lose any incentive to acknowledge the truth we are aware of, we struggle to reason with ourselves. This will cause us to align with whatever narrative shields us from the truth we believe is an enemy to getting what we want. The narrative can cause us to become lost in our denial, disregarding the evidence of our unconsciousness—that is often on display. Sometimes we prefer to remain lost in our own denial of reality, because we perceive truth as an enemy. We can compulsively protect the stagnation of our evolutionary idle, protecting our unconsciousness while forsaking our consciousness.

We have all been guilty of wanting our control pacified by the origins of our souls—*True Source Divine Origin Consciousness*. We create mind games that have us requesting our origins prove the value of truth to us. We determine if it is successful and normally assess this by the level of pacification, we believe we have received.

- Often mind games start with bargaining, such as "If I do this, my origins have to give me what I want," or "If I am given what I want, I will ....".

- Sometimes bargaining is a way of imposing responsibility for our actions on our origins, such as "If I am not stopped from doing ...., it means the deity I'm bargaining with approves," or "If I get away with my deception, it was meant to be."

Bargaining is created by our willingness to compete against our origins of truth and is usually done while taking no responsibility for our desire to control the origins of our souls. When the bargain works to our favour, we generally disregard the bargain, dismissing it as a thought with no conviction.

When life does not work to our plans, we can perceive our origins as the enemy. Is that fair? We don't even understand ourselves, so why do we think we know the best plan for our lives? Plans are stepping-stones. Events occur along the path, and outcomes are unpredictable. That is why we call it the journey of life. At any given moment, we can use our freewill to do anything. Sometimes we surprise ourselves with our own unpredictability.

Our origins—the divinity we come from—witnesses our choices and constantly creates opportunities for us to experience the depths of our soul truth. Life provides crossroads for our decisions, and our decisions create crossroads for ourselves and others.

Life is a collaborative event, and each action has a cause and effect—a ripple effect.

When we only seek to have our wants and desires pacified, it is easy to lose awareness of our natural synchronicity with truth. It also inhibits us from acknowledging the unconditional love and support the origins of our soul have for our self-discovery and evolutionary process.

Our origins do not compete against us—that is evident in our freewill. We choose the energy that vibrates or emanates off us; the truth of what we create is the energy our origins notice. It also reflects our soul maturity and emotional growth.

Truth is not something to command—it just is. The inherent value of energy cannot be underestimated. Unconscious energy is vibrational. Conscious energy has a pure frequency and is in harmony with truth. Each energy has its own signature and regardless of our acceptance of its reality, it is what it is.

- Manipulation is manipulation. The reasons why we use it may vary. How we attempt to hide the reality of it may differ. Irrespective of the why, how or intent, it is still manipulation.

- Kindness is kindness. How we decided to be of it may vary. How it is received may differ. Nevertheless, it is still kindness.

Truth is truth. We may struggle to realise what the truth is, but we cannot fool truth. We might be able to fool each other. We have either been unaware of the truth, altered our perceptions of what the truth is, or deliberately disregarded the truth.

The energy we use to motivate our actions is the truth we present to our origins—divinity. It is what we contribute to our lives, to life itself, and it's what we breathe into our relationships with others.

We decide if we value truth or disregard its value,
but truth never devalues or disregards itself.

CHAPTER THIRTEEN
When Did Authenticity Become the Enemy?

When we deny the truth of our behaviour and allow ourselves to act out the energy stored in our soul's unconsciousness, we exert a lot of effort into denying accountability and abrogating self-responsibility. This causes our relationships and interactions to become a quagmire of confusing emotional exchanges.

Evolution does not occur unless we take responsibility and accountability for our energy. This can be difficult because it requires us to own the truth of our behaviour—what we do with our freewill. We cannot control what others do to us, but we are responsible for what we do to ourselves.

Admitting the reality of our behaviour assists us in recognising our unconscious energy and that of others. It helps us unravel what has occurred in our lives that has left a residue of unconscious energy—carried unresolved emotions. It also enables us to examine the beliefs and fears that inhibit our acceptance of our own soul.

It can be difficult to acknowledge how reactive we are to another's behaviours. When we automatically react from our soul's unconsciousness, we can become so busy justifying our behaviours and reactions that we don't acknowledge the truth of them. However, recognising our unconscious energy is a stepping-stone to resolving it. Sometimes we are the victim, and other times we are the perpetuators. If we admit the reality of our emotions, behaviours and past experiences, we build a better understanding of the choices we make. We decide how we conduct ourselves or how we respond when we lose control of our own conduct. Sometimes others show us exactly what we wouldn't want to be.

Unconscious energy is identifiable because there is always an element of devaluing truth—devaluing the truth of what is occurring, purpose, and the intent. There is also a disregard for the cause and effect of the unconscious energy we use. Consequences are ignored.

For example, negative oppressive judgement, which is an unconscious energy:

- When we use negative oppressive judgement, we devalue any truth that interferes with the judgement we want to utilise. *We argue against truth even when we know it is true.*

- We do not speak of the purpose of being judgemental and deny the intent. *We don't say, "I'm doing this to make you feel inferior so I feel superior, and I am willing to play with all your insecurities to achieve reassurance that I am the most important in this verbal exchange."*

- We also ignore the consequence of misleading others and disregard how we make others feel with our judgement. *We justify ourselves with a narrative that makes us believe we are entitled. We deny the flow-on effect we instigate and become indifferent to the wake left behind our negative oppressive judgement.*

We use our many forms of unconscious energy to deceptively overshadow being aware of truth or to remain ignorant to truth. Truth is always at the foundation of any experience, feeling, or awareness. Any type of unconscious energy is constructed by our resistance to acknowledge the truth of something, such as the truth of ourselves, what we are doing, who we are affecting, our purpose, our intent, and the consequences of our decisions.

Imagine what it would be like if we all had to be honest about the what, why, and how we utilised unconscious energy—unresolved emotions.

29. Pick an unconscious energy: denial, indifference, manipulation, resentment, shame, greed, fear, sabotage, betrayal, judgement, or ....

a) When we use the unconscious energy of ...., how do we devalue truth?

....

....

b) What is it that we don't say when utilising ...?

....

....

c) What are the ignored consequences of using ....?

....

....

When we refuse to acknowledge the reality of the unconscious energy we use, we impair our ability to feel the purity of conscious energy. We create the shadows that shield us from feeling our own natural resonance with truth.

When we deny the importance of truth and our natural resonance with truth, we devalue conscious energy—the core essences of our souls, such as unconditional love, trust, integrity, and loyalty.

We can deceptively use the unconditional love, trust, integrity, and loyalty another has for us, as an opportunity to run the gauntlet of the energy of our soul's unconsciousness. We often choose this because we want to test our ability to have power and control over another, reality, and *True Source Divine Origin Consciousness.*

True Source Divine Origin Consciousness—**The origins of your soul—The birthplace of your existence—unconditionally loves you and is loyal to the process of the evolution of your soul.**

30. How have you reacted to this statement?

....

....

    a) Identify any unconscious energy—unresolved emotion—you use to reject unconditional love.

        ....

        ....

    b) Identify any conscious energy triggered by your acceptance of being unconditionally loved either by another, yourself, or your origins—*True Source Divine Origin Consciousness.*

        ....

        ....

31. Identify a time you exploited—used or purposely manipulated—another person.

....

....

    a)   What did you exploit? Their unconditional love for you, their trust, their integrity, or their loyalty.

        ....

        ....

    b)   What was the purpose of the exploitation or manipulation? What result did you want? What was the reason?

        ....

        ....

    c)   What was your intent? What were the stepping-stones? How did you think this was going to play out? Why did you believe this would provide you with what you wanted to happen? What were you prepared to forsake in your attempt to achieve the result you wanted?

        ....

        ....

    d)   What were the true consequences?

        ....

        ....

It is hard to look at the truth objectively. Even when you know it is true, you fear it exposes something you do not like to admit. If you don't challenge yourself, you cannot learn from your life experiences—the ones you instigate and the ones others bring to your door.

When we refuse to be honest with ourselves, we justify our behaviour and ignore our intent. This causes us to perceive life through the lens of ego, permitting ourselves to be indifferent to the true consequences of our actions. Ego means we are expressing our soul's unconsciousness. This also causes us to swing from arrogant beliefs of superiority, to beliefs of 'not being good enough'—inferior to those who seem to be able to control their image. Ego is a construct derived from our unconsciousness, and our own lack of awareness of our soul.

Ego is the self-image we create that camouflages
the true essence of our soul.

False self-images oppress our souls and
restricts our potential evolution.

We derive an illusion of power and control from our self-image—ego. As our reliance on our self-image expands, we develop a tolerance to our indifference to truth and begin to worship our desire for control. This illusion of power and control shields us from taking responsibility for our actions and leaves us obsessed with our own self-image. Paradoxically, we become overly concerned with how we are perceived by others, and everyone becomes a competitor. This detracts from our quality of life because we feel disconnected from our authenticity and are shallow in our relationships with others.

We lose connection to our authenticity because we pick and choose what we want to project and perform, instead of feeling and being an expression of our soul. Disconnection from our authenticity leaves us feeling miserable and aware of the void within. The void we feel within is an awareness of being separated and disassociated from our own authenticity; then we want to hide our awareness and gravitate to performing an image or uphold an illusion. This becomes a cyclic pattern of soul oppression.

If our self-image is intact, we believe we are in control and have power over our own reality. However, if our self-image is bruised, we deflate the ego and apply effort into being a victim of others' power and control. This can leave us with a victim mentality, developing a new image to perform. An image is not sustainable because it lacks the fundamentals of truth—it is not authentic.

Obsessing about our self-image enables narcissism, pride and vanity to take hold
and we lose awareness of the significance of who we naturally are
and how to significantly connect with others.

When protecting our self-image becomes a full-time preoccupation, we become obsessed with trying to pre-empt others' reactions and judgements in regard to us. We desire the power to control others' perception of us. This causes us to become performance-driven illusion creators, instead of being present in our own reality and aware of our own truth.

When we obsess about how our control, performances, and image are received by others, we become preoccupied with the potential judgement or known judgement of others. This causes us to spend a great deal of time and resources orchestrating the illusions that support what we want to convey. This affects what we buy, wear, talk about, and how we scale others with pecking orders. However, the fear of what could affect our display—images and illusions—deprives us of peace within. This can ignite constant mind chatter of assessing everything we do by how others may perceive it, which inhibits our ability to authentically interact with others, ourselves, truth, and life.

Instead of being authentic in our interaction with others, we become:

- Judgemental towards everyone, trying to uphold an illusion of superiority or sustain beliefs of inferiority.

- Phoney, deceptively looking for the angle to enhance one's own position—lacking integrity.

- A competitor to those admired, seeking to undermine them and their achievements.

- Rivals instead of supporters, we desire to weaken others—gradually or harshly.

- An opponent to those we live with, wanting to always be the superior one.

- A bully, intimidating those considered weaker or vulnerable.

- Shallow, lacking depth in our commitment to relationships.

- Superficial in the way we engage with life events.

- Posturers who pretend and have little substance.

- Anxiety ridden, seeking constant reassurance.

- Oppressors of others' shine of consciousness.

- Manipulators who hurt others—exploiters.

- Indifferent to truth.

- Acknowledge what your personal views are ....

....

The truth of how someone treats you becomes irrelevant to them,
if they choose for it to be irrelevant.

You cannot force them to hear, see, or feel the ramifications of their actions,
if they do not want to take responsibility for themselves.

You cannot debate, convince, or prove truth to those who reject being honest.
They have made their decision and you must do the same.

Decide to acknowledge what they refuse to and accept the relevance of your honesty.
Leave them to their denial and accept it is the path they chose;
then walk your own path with your integrity intact
and with peace in your heart.

Some people can become so consumed with their own judgement that they ignore facts and compulsively seek to secure their self-image or illusions. They have a narrative they want to execute and acknowledging the truth of their actions is not part of the story they tell themselves.

Sometimes it is the people you trust the most who teach you this lesson. You cannot control how another reacts and treats you; that is a decision they make. However, you decide if they continue to have the opportunity to treat you badly. When you know you are of worth and acknowledge the truth of how you are being treated, you begin to change what you choose to tolerate.

If you have been treated poorly, never allow that person to define your worth, because they cannot see through the fog of their own unconsciousness. Remember, if they aren't honest about themselves, they will not be honest about others. They do not know you as well as you know yourself. Never let another dictate what your awareness of truth should be. They can present evidence for you to contemplate, but don't give them the power to alter facts. If they couldn't accept the reality of who you are and what you did for them, they have chosen to devalue their relationship with you.

You don't treat those you love and respect poorly. Sometimes it is painful to accept evidence over what we want to believe. Acknowledge the truth of their behaviour and acknowledge the truth of your own.

Those who only see their own image assess people by how they enhance their image or distract from it. This causes them to become indifferent to how they treat those they judge as having no value to them, and someone is always left reeling in the wake of disappointment, hurt, and confusion. Those who seek authentic relationships assess people by how they feel in their presence, and they intentionally try not to be the source of disappointment, hurt, or confusion.

* 'When relationships are valued, they improve our life experience. A successful life is one of connection. It is those who we share life with, who enhance our time on earth. We all want our lives to have meaning, and it is through our relationships that we see, feel, and hear the cause and effect of our existence.'

*Excerpt from another title of the Insight and Awareness Anthology—Lorraine Nilon. Worthy of Recovery—Understanding the Wake Left Behind Life Shocks, Heartache, Betrayal, Abuse, Addiction and Narcissistic Relationships.

***Regardless of the relationship, enjoy it with the person who is there,
not the person you hope they will be.***

When we believe our self-image is of the utmost importance, we attempt to dictate how others should be when they are in our presence. Some people want love and friendship to be an arena to control and a place where they can act out the unconscious energy within them and dictate the response. They want those who love or care about them to be subservient and to never be held accountable for their own actions. This means they do not understand love or friendship, and their worship of control blinds them to the reality of what they eventually destroy—friendships, relationships, or loyalty.

When we worship our desire for control and fixate on our self-image, we begin to tell ourselves a narrative that exonerates us from self-responsibility. Within the narrative, we justify our lack of self-responsibility with blame, fault finding, and lies. We become lost in our deception and generate unconscious energy. For some, this becomes unadulterated narcissism and selfishness, and they delude themselves with their belief of entitlement. They lose touch with reality and attempt to exist in a bubble of their own creations. This means truth becomes their enemy and something they fear, and yet they seek to control it.

As our images and illusions entwine, we do not leave room for truth. When we fixate on upholding control over our own self-image and refuse to acknowledge the truth of our behaviour, beliefs, fears, and the words we speak, we crave validation for the image we portray. The validation we seek from others, causes us to be selective with our performances. Some will witness only what we deliberately portray, and others will be reserved to be the arena where we act out our inability to sustain the performed image, often unleashing our unbridled frustration upon them.

A classic example is how teenagers interact with their friends, as opposed to how they interact with their parents. Another is a narcissist interacting with those they want to impress, as opposed to how they treat their partner behind closed doors.

When we lose connection to our authentic self—our soul's consciousness—we build internal tension because we are trying to control our emotions, performance, others, and life. We hide from the truth of ourselves. This leaves us indentured to our illusion of control, tolerating our indifference to truth. Our indifference secures our deception which leads to manipulation. Control failure is always looming because we instinctively know we are living inauthentically, and it is our indifference, deception, and willingness to be manipulative that causes our illusion of control to fail.

***When we devalue truth and are willing to manipulate
those who love us, we become oppressors.***

Manipulators deceptively test those who love them with their willingness to be indifferent to truth. They delight in seeing how far they can go, without being held accountable for their behaviour. They become oppressors of truth because they have devalued it, and are only concerned with orchestrating the results they want. This causes them to betray truth, losing awareness of the significance of each individual soul. They deny the significance of honesty and compete against the truth of their experiences and own self-creations. This compromises their opportunity for evolution.

The way another chooses to treat you poorly is not a reflection of your worth. It is an expression of their disrespect for souls, truth, and self-responsibility. Acknowledging the behaviour of a manipulator, without filtering it through the fear of "Did I deserve it?" enables you to acknowledge their behaviour. This opens the door to making decisions that empowers you to learn from your experiences, and not to create self-definitions that shield you from your own truth.

When we devalue opportunities to acknowledge the energy of our own soul's unconsciousness, we lie to ourselves and discredit what we are aware of. We will use the protection of our self-image to supersede our awareness of our own behaviour or reactions. We will use our lies as reasoning, deceptively justifying our behaviour. The present opportunity for resolution and evolution is lost the minute we begin to lie to ourselves. Until we confront the lies we tell ourselves, we will be stuck in an evolutionary idle.

***We always have a reason behind what we do,
often a very unconscious reason,
but there is always a reason.***

If we are unwilling to explore the reasons why we do what we do, we become entrapped in our own evolutionary idle, fighting our awareness of truth and ignorant to our reality. This means we don't want to know the truth of our reality and prefer to align with the narrative we tell ourselves, which causes us to stalemate our own growth. It is easy to find ourselves stuck on our merry-go-round of soul oppression, repetitively acting out the energy of our soul's unconsciousness, clinging to the lies we tell ourselves. However, once we are aware of it, we have to decide for ourselves if we stay or start exploring how to resolve the issues holding us there.

Our merry-go-round of soul oppression is the never-ending cycle of oppressive interactions, events, and situations that sustain the energy of our soul's unconsciousness. Unless we acknowledge the reasons behind what we do and take self-responsibility, we will perpetuate the evolutionary idle that has movement without evolution.

To sustain the narrative we tell ourselves, we will attempt to secure not only our own, but often others' merry-go-round of soul oppression. We become willing to be the cause—the trigger—for another to act out their unconscious energy. We often exist in monotonous interplays and repetitive behaviours within our relationships with each other. We know the cause and effect of what we do to each other and compulsively trigger the perpetuation of emotional habits, verbal statements, or situations in which tedious events and interactions take place. When we exist on a merry-go-round of soul oppression, reoccurring emotional interactions, events, and situations occur, exposing the exact same energy. *This can be considered an opportunity to get real about yourself. Admit the truth of your own behaviour and how you contributed to whatever is familiar to you. You cannot change what you refuse to acknowledge, and it starts with the decision to do so.*

The narrative we want to tell ourselves,
so we can hide from the truth of our own behaviour,
becomes the path we walk, as we supply the energy to do so.

The narratives we tell ourselves that create beliefs of entitlement and justify our indifference, cause us to remain oppressed or fuel our readiness to oppress others. We use our awareness of others' unconsciousness—insecurities, desires, fears, negative beliefs, and resentments—as tools to ensure there is a conducive arena to act out what we find difficult to contain. This leaves us acting out our monotonous interplays and repetitive behaviours that expose the energy of our soul's unconsciousness. Our interactions with each other provide us with opportunities to either be of the energy of our unconsciousness or consciousness. Each decision has a cause and effect because we set energy in motion.

- Some people will justify the energy they act out from their soul's unconsciousness, but generally they are not as lenient for others.

- Some people will be lenient on other's acting out the energy of their soul's unconsciousness and not so for themselves.

The way we use our judgement determines who we are the hardest on, and our justifications become narratives that cause us to hide in our own fear of being truthful. This leaves us fearing truth, and truth becomes what we consider the enemy.

What you fear, you attack.
It will be the degree to which you choose to immerse yourself
in your indifference to truth that will determine the velocity of
your oppression of your own awareness of truth.

When we worship our self-image or our constructed illusion of reality, they become paramount to us. This leaves us operating from hidden agendas designed to pacify our desire for control. Paradoxically, we become possessed by a desire to pacify our own control and deprive ourselves of the freedom to be of our truth. This causes us to react to our life experiences intentionally unconscious because we have decided that truth is irrelevant, compared to the importance of our own desire to control our images and illusions.

Fixating on images and illusions corrupts our awareness and comprehension of
being a naturally significant, unique, independent, individual soul
of True Source Divine Origin Consciousness,
in the presence of other
naturally significant, unique, independent, individual souls
of True Source Divine Origin Consciousness.

When we lose our awareness of the equality of all souls, we start judging the value of others on their ability to enhance our images, secure our illusions, and pacify our desire for control. This means we lose the significance of our interaction with other souls. This deprives us of sharing our consciousness—the core essence of our souls with each other or feeling the truth of who we are.

Acknowledging that we have a choice is empowering. We exist in a field of infinite possibilities that all hinge on the choices we make.

We choose:

- When we get off the merry-go-round of soul oppression.

- When we are going to accept the true value of our souls.

- The importance of our relationships with others.

- How we share our energy with others.

- The legacy of our presence.

- Acknowledge what your personal views are ....
....

Choice creates freedom. What we do with this freedom always has a cause and effect on our souls. We have denied what we are indentured to within our soul's unconsciousness. Every time we lied to ourselves, we deprived ourselves of the core essences of our souls. We deprive ourselves of the freedom to be our authentic selves.

Acknowledging life as an opportunity to feel the significance of truth and trusting our soul journey so far has been for a purpose, opens the door to accepting the power of choice. Freewill is a creative force, and we should never lose sight of its importance.

We are unique, independent, individual souls who have an opportunity to share the truth of ourselves and our time with other souls. Choose wisely and with intent. Life is an opportunity to share time, while we all have freewill to determine what we individually bring to each present moment.

Freewill means you are a creator with your choices.
You decide if you are truthfully honest or deceptive with yourself
and this simple, yet complex decision determines how you interact with yourself,
which is the most important relationship you have.

CHAPTER FOURTEEN
When Did Love Become the Enemy?

We are souls in a physical body, and one of the most fundamental needs we have is to feel love and to love. We exist in this world through exchanges of energy, and the ones who nurture our souls make us feel alive.

Unconditional love is difficult to define. It is an emanation from the core of our being that expresses a natural force that is undefinable and yet essential to our wholeness. Our love for each other and ourselves creates exchanges of energy that nurture our souls. It cannot be constructed; there is no artificial substitute, and in its purest form it is undeniable.

We communicate in many forms. It is an exchange of actions that stem from decisions, such as the words, looks, movements, ideas, and energy we choose as our actions. Our interactions, whether walking past each other or spending time together, create an exchange of energy. When we are of our core essences, the exchange is nurturing. *A simple smile or a thank you, can have a heart-warming effect.* However, if there is a lack of love and respect within our exchanges, it hurts us and makes us feel insignificant. When there is a withdrawal from the core essences of our souls, we use our unconscious energy to replace them. This causes our exchanges of energy to be oppressive in some form. *A judgemental look or snatching our change from a shopkeeper because we are in a hurry can have a dispiriting affect.*

Unconditional love is unified core essences. Each strand is significant and an emanation of our souls' purity. Kindness has a profound effect. Kindness unified with patience, joy, compassion, and .... is a form of unconditional love. Unconditional love comes in many combinations, and it is a natural response of unifying the core essences that express the truth of what we feel in that moment. It is the natural force of our divinity and is expressed from the purity of our soul's consciousness.

- Unconditional love stems from the willingness to commit to being of the core essences of our souls and the intent to share them with ourselves and others.

- Indifference stems from the willingness to commit to opposing, denying, and overriding the core essences of our souls and the intent to oppress others and ourselves.

The core essences of your soul include unconditional love,
which is the unification of all core essences.

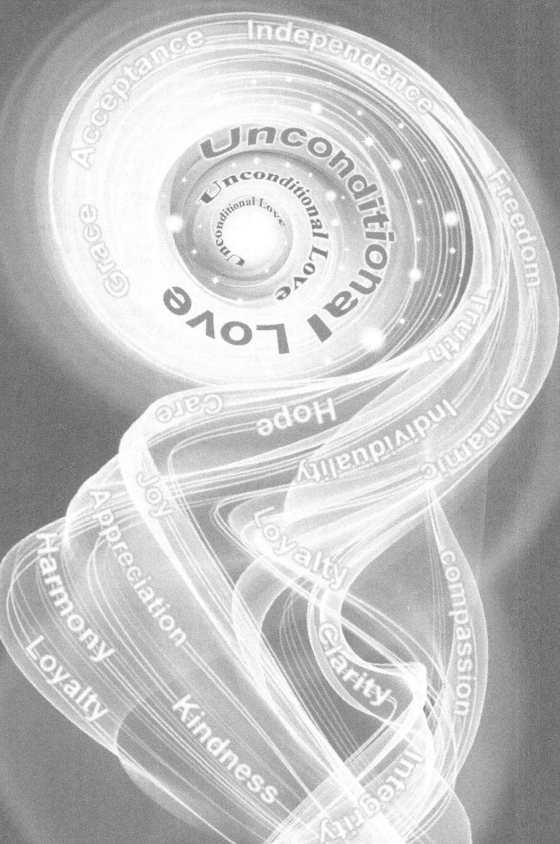

When we lose awareness of unconditional love within ourselves, we forget that it's part of our natural selves. We conjure concepts about love we use to avoid confronting, whatever impedes our love for our own soul—self-love. This affects our ability to love and to accept the love of others.

How we love our children, parents, siblings, partners, friends, and pets, all differ. However, when unconditional love is the foundation, we feel the nurturing of our soul and of those we love. Being either the giver or the receiver of unconditional love nurtures the souls of all involved.

When we separate from our awareness of our own soul, we create a distorted perception of ourselves that morphs into beliefs about our lovability or deters us from freely expressing the love within our soul. The distortions are as varied as people. Some stem from our history of abuse or exploitation. Most of these distortions entwined with fears that morph into negative self-judgements. Sometimes we don't even realise they are distortions, and we will go out of our way to ensure the beliefs entwined with negative self-judgement remain intact.

When we disassociate from feeling our resonance with truth, it is easy to devalue the essence of unconditional love. This causes us to undervalue the importance of our relationships and of feeling connected with whom we share our life experiences. All our relationships have meaning, regardless of the form—family, romantic, partnerships, friendships, colleagues, or acquaintances—because it is where we exchange energy. What we offer and what we are willing to receive reveals a lot about our soul maturity.

How honest we are with ourselves affects the way we love. How we love and the way we treat those who love us is important for us to acknowledge. What we do to love, regardless of the type of relationship, always exposes what we attempt to hide within our soul's unconsciousness.

We attempt to hide our:

- Fears
- Denials
- Jealousies
- Ignorance
- Arrogance
- Selfishness
- Insecurities
- Slothfulness
- Resentments
- Competitiveness

- Non self-reflection
- Indifference to truth
- Unresolved emotions
- Suppressed memories
- Beliefs of unworthiness
- The desire to have control of another
- Acknowledge what your personal views are ....
- ....

This list is as varied as people.

Being loving requires us to be present and to deal with our unresolved emotions—the energy of our soul's unconsciousness. Loving relationships are opportunities to deal with the hidden recesses of our unconsciousness because we care about how we affect the ones we love. Our love creates opportunities to resolve what impacts others and ourselves. When we intentionally choose not to hurt one another, it reflects our love and respect not only for them but also for ourselves. Love and respect is also something we need to accept we deserve for ourselves from others.

We can be very loving towards others and neglect ourselves. Self-love is making the effort to resolve the battlefield in our mind about our self-worth. It is accepting we are naturally significant, and life is the arena where we get to choose how we treat ourselves and others.

Try acknowledging when it is a struggle to be truthful. It is your truthfulness that reconnects your awareness to your soul, so your consciousness out shines your unconsciousness. The core essences are soul expressions—consciousness shining.

Regardless of who you are and what you have experienced, you deserve to reconnect, recover, and rejuvenate.

Reconnect with the meaningfulness of your own existence.
Recover from the wounds you carry, and
rejuvenate the way you interact with life.

Your relationship with your soul, deserves to be acknowledged as the most important relationship you have.

If we individually recognise this,
we'd interact with the core essences of our souls,
such as integrity, kindness, and compassion.

This will make the world a better place.

You are in an evolutionary process, and you will be confronted with many emotional upheavals. Others will disappoint you. However, if you remain respectful of yourself and value the core essences of your soul, you will learn from these experiences instead of being consumed by the energy they attempt to use to oppress you.

You will also disappoint yourself. Acknowledge the cause, remain respectful of yourself, and don't tell yourself a story justifying or defending putting yourself down. Instead consider the following options:

- Reset your mind-set. See what has occurred as an opportunity to objectively observe yourself.

- Readapt to your new awareness, and change your approach.

- Reaffirm you are worthy of self-love and an evolving soul—evolving through reconnaissance and truthfulness.

- Realign with the core essences of your soul and nurture yourself through the experience.

- Refocus your intent. Seek to understand and operate with commitment to being of your truth.

- *Reconnect, Recover and Rejuvenate.*

32. Reconnect with ....

....

33. Recover from ....

....

34. Rejuvenate your ....

....

When self-love is valued and nurtured, it makes it easier to deal with the parts of ourselves that do not reflect our true intent or nature.

***Unconditional love stems from the willingness to share
the best of ourselves with ourselves and others.***

Love is not an invitation to dump what we cannot contain, nor is it an excuse to deny self-responsibility. Love is not permission to become another's dumping ground for the unresolved emotions they refuse to address. When we allow ourselves to accept another's indifference towards us or are willing to be indifferent to the cause and effect of our own behaviour, we devalue love and start to erode the relationship, whether we realise it or not. When we become indifferent to ourselves, we devalue the relationship we have with ourselves, and this always has a flow-on effect into our relationships with others.

Our indifference towards the truth of ourselves causes us to lose insight into the authenticity of unconditional love, so we chase what we believe love is or should be. We also compare another's love for us with what we desire it to be. This can leave us devaluing another's love or exploiting it.

The authenticity of love matters, because love feeds our souls.

Our beliefs of what love should be can leave us very disappointed in others. We can be unrealistic or too eager to settle for less than we deserve, in the pursuit to feel loved. We often put too high an expectation on love, and instead of seeing who or what we love, we create filters of what we expect in return for our love. This distorts love, and it becomes tainted with the burdens we attach to it. This doesn't mean we don't love—we just give our love a purpose, which takes away from the purity of unconditional love. This purpose differs for each of us because it depends on:

- What we want to take from it.

- What we want in the present moment.

- What we hope to achieve in the long run.

- Our expectations of how we should feel and experience love.

- Our beliefs about being entitled to act out our unconsciousness.

- Acknowledge what your personal views are ....

....

Unconditional love doesn't come with a result-driven purpose;
it is an expression of being witness to the significance of another and ourselves.

We often confuse love with infatuation, idealisms, sacrifice, lust, pity, codependency, and obligation.

35. What would you like to add to the list?

We often confuse love with ....

It's important to recognise tainted love or any confusion around love. The confusion is an awareness that it is time to be honest with ourselves and with each other. If we refuse to be honest, we align with illusions and the narrative we tell ourselves that justify our denial. This means when the illusion bursts, or when the narrative we want no longer applies, we discard those we once claimed to love, often without recognising that we were loving for a purpose, not unconditionally.

We can seek an illusion of love and become willing to disregard the reality of how we feel and what we are experiencing. The illusion of love can morph into beliefs, control structures, and performed images, but none of these feed our souls. Unconditional love is felt; it doesn't come with a to-do list.

Acknowledging the beliefs, judgements, and fears that inhibit us from feeling the purity of unconditional love within ourselves, others, and of our origins opens the door to examining what is unresolved within ourselves. *You are a soul worthy of love. This includes self-love.*

If you have done something that makes you believe you are unlovable, take full responsibility for it and apologise with sincerity. Be the person you wished you were at the time. Learn from it; don't wallow in it.

If someone has done something to you that made you feel unworthy of love, reclaim the reality of being worthy. No one has the right to tell you, your worth. Their actions and words are an expression of themselves, and they have exposed their unconsciousness, not your worthiness.

Be careful not to adopt what they have hurtfully done or said as a self-definition or as the foundation for your beliefs about life and people. If you already have, you have some resolving to do. Give yourself permission to acknowledge reality and recognise that anyone who treats people poorly is not an authority of anybody's worth. They exposed their indifference to truth and to the opportunity to be loved by you. Consciously acknowledge you are in a recovery process with the intent to evolve from the oppression you feel.

The following help us to recognise opportunities to be honest with ourselves:

- Accept reality.

- Acknowledge what has occurred and the residue of unconscious energy left in its wake.

- Appraise what can be learned, instead of judging it. Judgement holds you in the duality—right-wrong, good-bad—and you can get stuck on a see-saw of self-judgement that creates an evolutionary idle.

- Appreciate that you have the intent to resolve and evolve, and everyone chooses their own path.

Love nurtures you through the process of resolving and evolving; however, you have to choose this as your approach. You have to choose to treat yourself as someone you love.

Love cannot be bought, sold, or traded. We cannot make someone love us the way we want them to. Love is a presence that can be felt, and the more present and honest we are, the more we recognise it.

Sometimes our desire to dictate what love is causes us to miss an opportunity to feel the dynamics of love, which overshadows the reality of the experience. Love nurtures our souls, which assists in our own emotional and spiritual growth, especially with regards to self-love.

Our misconceptions about ourselves can leave us stuck in an evolutionary idle, waiting for another to announce our worth because they have decided to love us. This means we have fixated on the belief that another's love determines our worth. *Someone who truly loves you knows you are of worth—this is true. However, if you don't have love for yourself, their love is not going to give you what you crave. You crave feeling the truth of your soul and the purity of your unconditional love flowing within the core of your being. You also yearn to share this with others.*

Our rejection of the value of love causes us to compromise our own integrity, and we become reluctant to acknowledge our contributions to our relationships. When we deny the reality of how we treat or how we allow another to treat us, we fixate on the narratives we tell ourselves and gloss over reality. This has a cause and effect on our boundaries and on how we feel about ourselves, whether we acknowledge it or not.

The more you value yourself, the healthier your boundaries are.

Healthy boundaries represent valuing truth. We intrinsically know truth is significant and important to our wellbeing. We expect each other to be truthful, and yet we ignore the known lies we tell ourselves. It is our lack of self-love and self-worth that sustains the lies we tell ourselves. This keeps us in cyclic patterns that oppress our awareness of our truth.

When love becomes something we want to control, we lose the authenticity of love and devalue being truthful. We can even weaponize it, using affection as a reward and withdrawing our love as punishment. This requires us to overturn our integrity and operate with conditions derived from our wants, desires, and expectations. Our conditions take over our abilities to objectively observe ourselves, which leads to more demands and a rejection of truth. This is not love; it is dictatorship. Love is sharing, not ownership. Love is not a reward for conforming to the conditions set by another. It is a soul-to-soul recognition of valuing the existence of another, knowing the relationship enriches both lives and souls.

When we devalue integrity and disconnect from acknowledging and resonating with the unconditional love we have for truth, we become lost in our soul oppression. This causes us to become entangled in the images and illusions we perform that secure our denial of ourselves. When we lose our integrity, all we offer are unsustainable images and illusions. We also disregard what we sacrifice, as we attach to an illusory control of love and life.

Defending images and illusions cause us to disengage from the truth of being unconditionally loving and unconditionally loved by our origins—*True Source Divine Origin Consciousness*. We abandon the truth of our awareness of our soul and seek another to fill the void we feel, separating from our awareness of ourselves and disassociating from our truth. This can create a lot of dilemmas and conundrums within our relationships and interactions with each other. We attempt to give each other the responsibility of filling the void created by our denial. No one else can fill this void. They can inspire us, but filling the void is our responsibility. It's filled by knowing and loving ourselves. This can be motivated and enhanced by another's love, but they cannot do the inner-work required to resolve the void we feel.

Unconditional love is a core essence that enables us to trust ourselves to feel divinity. The energy of divinity is always with us; it is found in truth and is truth.

Unconditional love is the natural energy of *True Source Divine Origin Consciousness*. *True Source Divine Origin Consciousness* encourages and waits for us to acknowledge and trust the truth of our soul's consciousness. Trust stems from the choice to do so.

Our trust in truth becomes a stepping-stone to the resolution of our unresolved emotions. We individually decide how we value truth. Truth does not make us value it. Sometimes it is undeniable, and sometimes there is too much evidence to hide truth, but it takes a decision on our part to acknowledge its value.

When we decide truth is valuable, we discover the significance of being truthful. Our truthfulness creates a platform that can be shared—a meeting place of connection. Unconscious energy, regardless the type, never offers connection. When we value truth, we realise unconscious energy does not flow. It is sporadic, contradictory, cyclic, unsubstantial, confusing, and ... When love feels this way, it has been tainted with unconscious energy, which can become harmful and leaves a wake of mixed emotions.

Truthfulness is a bridge to unifying with our origins.
Unconditional love is the connector, and our truthfulness
clears the debris of our own unconsciousness.

You are a unique, independent, individual soul of *True Source Divine Origin Consciousness*. Mankind has many labels, beliefs, and ideas concerning our origins. Our soul's consciousness holds the connection to our origins, and unifying with our own consciousness reconnects us to our origins. *How you choose to do this reveals the uniqueness of your soul, the independence of your choices, and the individuality of your insight and awareness.*

- Mankind is who we are when we forget we are souls.

- Humanity is who we are when we operate from our souls.

Our origins are presently beyond our full comprehension, but we can choose to explore— to open our eyes and hearts, and examine what oppresses our unconditional love. *True Source Divine Origin Consciousness,* does not align with our illusory control of life; its energy is in the truth of our reality.

When we choose to trust in our uniqueness, we are choosing to experience the truth of ourselves. We feel freedom when we do this without a controlled expectation anchoring us to the familiarity of our own or mankind's control structures. At the core of our being, we want to resolve the unconscious energy that separates and disassociates us from feeling our truth and the significance of our souls.

We often struggle against our natural significance because we want to control what is significant, which incites us to judge, compare, or be envious. This has us devaluing our soul, inhibiting us from discovering, exploring, and accepting our own natural significance.

Denied significance has consequences. It causes us to compulsively revert to the cyclic pattern of our soul oppression. When we choose to protect our soul oppression, we fertilise the fears and beliefs that sustain our self-rejection. This inhibits us from recognising ourselves as naturally significant souls of *True Source Divine Origin Consciousness*, and we lose awareness of our uniqueness, independence, and individuality. This causes us to struggle in our opposition to accept life as an opportunity to discover the relevance of our insight and awareness. Instead, we align with justifying our judgement. Unfortunately, our negative self-judgement is the first behaviour we justify, putting ourselves down and deepening the layers of our soul's unconsciousness.

Opposing our own uniqueness, independence, and individuality has consequences, all of which cause us to anchor to the familiarity of our soul oppression. We remain in cyclic patterns of soul oppression, utilising our unconscious energy and ignoring the core of our being.

When we unconditionally love and accept the reality of our significance as a soul, we create an opportunity to evolve beyond our denial of our own uniqueness, independence, and individuality. This has the following consequences:

- Our understanding and awareness expand.

- We recognise life has purpose and is meaningful.

- Unconditional love is acknowledged as a strength.

- We get real about soul maturity and spiritual growth.

- We reconnect with our own awareness of being eternal souls.

- We feel connected to our origins—*True Source Divine Origin Consciousness*.

- We intently participate in the discovery of both our conscious and unconscious energy.

- Acknowledge what your personal views are ....

....

....

Self-love is a bridge to discovering what is unresolved. It is a way to nurture ourselves through the shock of what we have done with our freedom of choice—freewill. We can also become shocked by what we have done to others or realise what has been done to us.

When we are unwilling to acknowledge truth, we control ourselves to resist, deny, and avoid the:

- Truth of ourselves.

- Cause and effect of what we do.

- Truth of our reality.

- Truth of another.

Truth is hidden under our unwillingness to be honest, waiting for us to realise what is true.

36. We have the freedom to ignore our awareness of truth, but what does that actually enhance? Does it pacify our control, sustain illusions, or improve our image?

....

....

We cannot alter what truth is—we can only conceal truth from ourselves with deception. When we are willing to deceive ourselves, we emotionally see-saw within the duality of our judgement and create a toxic game with beliefs about our wants, desires, and expectations. If we cannot get the results we want, these morph into desires for control or leave us believing we are a victim. This causes us to stagnate within our cyclic patterns of soul oppression.

We control ourselves to be victims of our own control.
Our desire for control always results in us feeling oppressed.
Control energy has an insatiable appetite and is rarely pacified.

When we become codependent on our soul oppression, we reject truth, resulting in irrational behaviour. When we believe we are in control of life, we deny reality, resulting in irrational behaviour. Unfortunately, we often perceive truth and love as the enemy—something that is going to deprive us of what we believe is more valuable than truth or love.

What is perceived as more valuable than truth or love differs from person to person, but there are themes that morph into beliefs. For some:

A. It's the illusion of safeguarding themselves from being hurt, so they can create the illusion of being in control of their vulnerability. *"Love hurt me before, I'm not giving it a chance to do it again."* This leaves them feeling disconnected, unloved, and vulnerable to judgement.

B. It's also the fear of losing something. *"If I acknowledge truth, I will lose my denial—my protection—that shields me from what I fear I cannot cope with. I don't need love, just the illusion of security."* This often leaves them protective of their own misery and loneliness.

C. It is the addiction to self-pity. *"I'm unlovable, no one wants me."* This leaves them wallowing in their self-indulgence, refusing to accept reality.

D. It is desiring control over their perceptions. *"My judgement is truth. If others do what I want, I will love them. If they don't, I'm not wasting my time, or I will pull them into line with punishment."* This approach leaves them narcissistically conducting their interactions with others.

E. It is ....

    " .... "

    This leaves them ....

    You'll use this response in question 41.

37. What have you tried to safeguard that caused you to devalue truth or love?

....

....

a) How do you feel about your answer?

....

....

b) What have you learnt from this experience?

....

....

c) Identify any fears or beliefs you have uncovered.

....

....

38. What have you feared losing that caused you to devalue truth or love?

....

....

a) How do you feel about your answer?

....

....

b) What have you learnt from this experience?

....

....

c) Identify any beliefs and fears?

....

....

39. What have you been addicted to that caused you to devalue truth or love?

....

....

    a)   How do you feel about your answer?

        ....

        ....

    b)   What have you learnt from this experience?

        ....

        ....

    c)   Identify any beliefs and fears?

        ....

        ....

40. What did you want control over that caused you to devalue truth or love?

....

....

    a)   How do you feel about your answer?

        ....

        ....

    b)   What have you learnt from this experience?

        ....

        ....

    c)   Identify any beliefs and fears?

        ....

        ....

41. What have you learnt from your response to E? Has any of it caused you to devalue truth or love?

....

....

    a) How do you feel about your answer?

        ....

        ....

    b) What have you learnt from this experience?

        ....

        ....

    c) Identify any beliefs and fears?

        ....

        ....

⊷⊷⊷†⊶⊶⊶

When truth has no value to us, we become indifferent to those we hurt in our pursuit to secure our beliefs. This causes us to do, say, and become somebody we don't like. We also become intentionally unconscious, arrogantly or ignorantly operating without contemplation or empathy while overriding our own awareness.

- Arrogance means we don't care about truth and claim we already know what is important.

- Ignorance means we don't want to know the truth and prefer to remain uninformed.

When we force ourselves to be intentionally unconscious, we manipulate truth. We allow ourselves to act-out behaviours that are meant to conceal reality. For this to occur, we need others to align with our wants so we can justify our rejection of truth, reality, and at times, love. It is hard to remain intentionally unconscious in the presence of another's love for us, so we seek to destroy either their love or the awareness of being loved.

The following describe being intentionally unconscious:

- We become the orchestrator of oppression, putting others down and seeking to undermine their perception of themselves.

- We construct a convoluted web of deception, believing we can validate ourselves by justifying the lies we spin.

- We embody the unconscious energy—such as indifference, nastiness, selfishness, jealousy, and .... We oppose and judge others when we recognise their unconscious energy, but justify our own.

- We fabricate a story, so we can deny our reality.

When we elect to be intentionally unconscious, we choose to miss the opportunities to resolve the unresolved emotions that sustain our own soul oppression; instead, we utilise them. Intentionally unconscious means we refuse to be reflective, to openly discuss, to take responsibility or to empathise with the cause and effect of our actions and reactions. This inhibits us from unconditionally loving to our full potential.

We can never control truth.
We can only control ourselves to be deceptive,
and deny being aware of truth.

We often lie to ourselves so we can bypass the process of resolution and evolution of our soul oppression. We want to remain intentionally unconscious because we are willing to hide from the truth of our soul and our origins. This leaves us worshipping the illusion of control, and our willingness to love becomes a casualty of it. Love is often sacrificed in pursuit of securing control of our lies, beliefs, and demands.

When we encase ourselves in the energy that oppresses us, it is our refusal to be honest with ourselves that sustains the oppression.

- Truthfulness is found in love—love for ourselves, others, and truth.

- Dishonesty exposes our lack of love for ourselves, others, and truth.

We embed these beliefs in the root of our soul's unconsciousness—our soul-denial. The crux of our soul's unconsciousness has become a vault for our embedded beliefs and fears of truth. This causes us to be enslaved by the repetitive nature of our soul-denial history. We encase ourselves in the unconscious energy that protects the denial of our soul, which often makes our truth an enigma. It requires self-love to truly resolve the source of our own soul oppression.

We control our soul incarceration by justifying and vindicating the energy of our soul's unconsciousness, especially our desire for control. When we defiantly oppose exploring, accepting, and resolving the reality of our own unconscious energy, we inhibit our ability to love ourselves.

When we defy any truth that interferes with our desire for control, our illusion of having control, or even our beliefs of being unable to gain control, we keep truth as our enemy. Our defiance is the source of many beliefs, one of which is that truth is the enemy. To resolve any embedded belief or fear, we have to be willing to acknowledge the significance of truth.

> *Loving ourselves makes the process of resolution and evolution easier,*
> *but it does not annul the process.*

Defiance is an unresolved emotion and a control structure when it results in oppression. When it is inverted into conscious energy, it becomes commitment, respectful determination, and spirited enthusiasm. Inverting our defiance requires conscious awareness and willingness to follow through with our actions. Understanding a concept but not practising it, does not result in spiritual growth. Evolution and awoken consciousness require us to love ourselves, while we support ourselves through our unique spiritual journey.

- When we retreat to our known patterns of soul oppression, we have the option to truly acknowledge what we are doing to ourselves. Evolution occurs through being truthful about what we are doing to ourselves and others.

- Acknowledging our unresolved emotions, starts with the decision to do so. This is choosing to be diligently aware that evolution occurs through the acknowledgement of our soul's consciousness and unconsciousness.

- Feeling and accepting our awareness of our soul truth creates a path that will end in resolution and evolution.

- We must acknowledge and accept responsibility for our freedom of choice. Acceptance of freewill opens the door to self-acceptance—unconditionally loving our own uniqueness.

- Recognising our independence enables us to embrace the significance of our souls.

- We must embrace life as an opportunity to evolve our souls.

We are the opportunity for evolution. Consciously participating in the exploration of truth stems from the choice to do so. When we acknowledge the truth of our contribution to our own emotional, energetic, and physical reality, we uncover our ability to recognise our own soul and the presence of *True Source Divine Origin Consciousness*, because we are being truthful with ourselves.

To liberate yourself from your soul oppression, you have to accept your internal knowing, and choose to unconditionally love the truth of your soul. Your soul's consciousness is the part of you that seeks to live the true essence of your soul. You are a naturally significant, unique, independent soul, who has the ability to trust that life creates opportunities for exploration of the truth of your soul.

Freedom stems from constantly deciding to accept truth is not the enemy. When you acknowledge truth was never the enemy, you understand the enemy of your soul has always been fear.

We have been programmed to fear what we don't understand,
and we don't understand the truth of ourselves.

When you acknowledge truth was never the enemy, your honest exploration of truth liberates you from how you oppress the truth of who you are. Discovering what resonates with your soul is worth the journey. Give yourself permission to use the core essences of your soul as the bridge to your evolution.

Acknowledged truth is never the enemy; it is an expression of our humanity.
Acknowledged truth is choosing to unconditionally love the
consciousness of our souls and our collective origins.

HONEST
EFFORT
REQUIRED

SECTION 5

Your soul journey is an opportunity to learn to trust the true essence of who you are, without being encumbered by your illusions of yourself and your denial of reality, both of which caused some of your unresolved emotions in the first place.

Conclusion

Exploring your spirituality is a fascinating and frustrating adventure. It is an ongoing expedition throughout your entire life. Spirituality is about doing the inner work required to evolve. This means getting real and honest with yourself.

Psychologist Carl Jung wrote, "People will do anything, no matter how absurd, to avoid facing their own souls". Spirituality means facing our souls and acknowledging the absurd so you can deal with it. When we venture in with integrity, to explore what we have suppressed and denied, we leave the exploration with confidence and appreciation for our own honesty. Facing our soul is not a one-off event; it's a continuous part of our spirituality and evolution.

Awakened consciousness is not a destination to arrive at or a level to reach; it's accepting life as an evolutionary process. This is the purpose of life. Many of us know we were born with an evolutionary purpose. Some of us look for someone to tell us our life purpose. They feel the internal yearning, and they think if they could just find it and get on with it, they would feel free. The problem is they are often looking for something or someone that is going to enable them to bypass having to deal with what is suppressed. No such luck—it doesn't work this way. You can fool yourself for a while, but when it crashes, it will leave you feeling lost, wallowing in the energy of your unconsciousness.

I have witnessed many gallant attempts to bypass the process of honest exploration, resolving, and maturing. I've seen many with impressive yet shallow images perform as if they were evolved. However, perfecting suppression, and performing an image is not spiritual growth. Images end with a lot of disappointment and tears. For some they turn their tears into laughter as they recognise the absurdity of what they have done to deny their own unresolved emotions. Others get stuck, defending and repeating patterns with awareness and forced denial. This is never pretty. Stripping away an illusion and dismantling beliefs is frightening, but being stuck should scare us more.

Evolution means to learn, grow, and evolve with new awareness and understanding. This does not occur when we protect what we need to resolve. We spend more effort on avoiding our emotions than we do on dealing with them, and the avoidance causes us the most grief. When we accept we seek to be of our truth, and an image isn't going to feed our soul; we can also embrace the rise and falls of the evolutionary process. This enables our understanding of our soul journey to expand.

The number one rule for recognising you are an evolving soul is to have a sense of humour. *You are going to need it.* We go to great lengths to protect our unconsciousness, and you will surprise yourself. Knowing this is part of the process, helps us to recognise when it's time to honestly look at ourselves.

There is one fundamental purpose we all have, and that is to resolve the unconscious energy we created that separates us from the truth of who we are.

You were not born to "find yourself". You were born to resolve the emotional baggage that does not reflect the truth of your soul. You were born to unify your soul—to be whole—and to resolve the energy you created that cannot reside in the frequency of truth. Awakening to your own consciousness means you are prepared to take responsibility for your spiritual growth and soul maturity. It requires action that stems from truthfulness, not just belief.

Spiritual wellbeing has such a flow-on effect to how you live and interact with others, and to the legacy you leave to this world. Some of us are already aware we were born to resolve our unconsciousness, and some have been so impacted by what has occurred to them that resolution is part of their survival plan. Others will awaken to the evolutionary purpose as their curiosity builds. Our soul maturity is the result of our spirituality, evolution, and awakened consciousness, and we each have a unique path to walk, looking for the clues that will enable us to face all the aspects of our soul.

Our soul's purpose can be summed up with the words of the ancient Greek philosopher, Socrates: "Know thy self". It has been written about for centuries, and it is still fundamental to our soul maturity.

I hope this book has ignited your curiosity, and I hope it has been a rewarding adventure of reading, contemplation, and discussion. This book is like a good road map—it points you in a direction, but you are the traveller.

Contemplation cultivates an inner connection,
an awareness of yourself.

Glossary

Divinity: Our origin. The core of our souls and existence. The eternal purity of unconditional love. Free of any form of deception. Free of unconscious energy. Purity of truth.

Duality of judgement: A dual state, contrasting, complementing, or opposing each other. The activation and sustainability of emotionally seesawing between two mindsets, opinion, or justifications.

Evolution: The process of change resulting from taking responsibility for resolving the unconscious energy of your soul's unconsciousness. Evolution is the process of embracing the truth of who you are and operating from the purity of your soul. Evolution stems from accepting truth, caring for and valuing your relationship with your soul.

Evolutionary idle: Also called *energetic idle*. Generated limbo from the process of fighting against truth in an attempt to have control. The action of using your control structures to fight for dominance over truth, which can be physically felt as an internal vibration and recognised as being stuck on an emotional merry-go-round.

Evolutionary idle describes being in the energy of your soul's unconsciousness and denying your awareness of what can be felt or observed. It is allowing yourself to protect the stagnation created by your indifference to truth, denying yourself an opportunity for resolution and evolution to occur.

Energy is moving but there is no developmental growth in understanding.

Image of consciousness: An imitation of what you believe to be consciousness. Using superficial and egotistical facades and charades to try to depict spiritual elitism as you seek to be revered, while denying the truth of your own deception and manipulation. A control structure orchestrated by your willingness to be dishonest in your relationship with truth.

A performance with the intent to be indifferent to the purity of truth. The belief that you are entitled to dictate what truth is to yourself and others, to ensure you remain on top of what you perceive as a spiritual pecking order.

Deception cloaked in the illusion of spirituality.

Judgement: One of the barriers to truth within your soul's unconsciousness, used to oppress your awareness of your soul's consciousness. Judgement is a binding force of your embedded beliefs, fears, and desire for control that you use to incite and sustain your own soul oppression or the oppression of others.

Judgement inhibits your ability to feel truth. It is used to oppose and deflect your resonance with truth.

Judgement is a catalyst that fuels the connection between the different unresolved emotions within your soul's unconsciousness and ignites your indifference to truth.

Limbo: A state of being disregarded or forgotten. Trapped in a state of uncertainty.

Merry-go-round of soul oppression: A repetitive cyclic emotional, behavioural, energetic, or physical pattern that leaves you feeling disconnected from your soul.

Resolution: To find a solution to a problem. The energy of your soul's unconsciousness is problematic for your soul's consciousness. Resolution is the decision to bring yourself back to truth. The critical foundation for resolution is the willingness to take responsibility to understand the truth. The determination to resolve is what helps you evolve.

Soul accountability: Recognising and taking into consideration the cause and effect of what you do to the eternalness of your soul.

Soul journey: The eternal journey of your soul. This lifetime is part of the expedition to discover the true essence of soul and to unify with freewill, to the consciousness flowing within your soul and of your origins of truth—*True Source Divine Origin Consciousness*. Traveling toward enlightenment—to know thy self.

Soul maturity: Developed self-awareness and a willingness to take responsibility for your soul. Still in the transitional stage of evolution, but it is with conscious participation, acceptance of reality, and engagement with truth. To be aware of the purpose, intent, and consequences of your actions and to make decisions based on this awareness.

Spiritual bypassing: Ignoring the reality of yourself, while clinging to a spiritual belief or illusion that distracts you from being honest. Using spiritual concepts, words, and beliefs to deny self-responsibility and soul accountability.

Spiritual growth: Reconnecting and expanding your relationship with the truth of who you are. Broadening your understanding and awakening to the consciousness within. Resolving the concepts, beliefs, thoughts, and fears that inhibit your freedom to be your authentic self. Integrating what you learn and what resonates with your soul into your day-to-day existence. It is part of the process of evolution.

Symphony of truth: The reality of life. The truth of all energy creating and contributing to reality and a present moment.

Acknowledgements

I am humbled and grateful for the support I've received from my family and friends. I sincerely appreciate all the thoughtful encouragement I've experienced along the way.

I have had the good fortune of having people around me who wholeheartedly offer their assistance, and I am thankful for all the ways they enrich my life. It means so much to me that they have faith in me, the significance of this book, and my other projects.

A special thank you to:

Katherine Close – Illustrator.

I love working with you. I am constantly amazed by your talent, insight, and integrity. Your artistic gift enriches the quality of my books and I am so profoundly grateful to be a beneficiary of your expertise.

David Baker – Editor.

I am impressed by your conscientious approach and value the thoughtfulness shown.

Tim Williams – Developmental Editor.

I am truly grateful for all your support and thoroughly enjoyed our collaborative process through-out the development of this book.

Rachel Dearnely, Dominque Williams and Fran Rockliffe – Proofreaders.

I sincerely appreciate all the effort applied to catching mistakes and providing thoughtful suggestions.

Leanne McIntyre-Burnes, Amber and Carley Hennessy and to my mate Will for assisting my clarity.

I appreciate the candid responses to my "tossing ideas around" conversations, your time, and attention.

Neil and Tammy Howell for supporting and bringing a fresh approach to my endeavours.

Words cannot express the heartfelt gratitude I have for all those who enrich my life and are so supportive.

Finally thank you to the readers—fellow explorers—
I hope you enjoyed your exploration.

Your opinion of this book matters and your honest review may help others find it.

All reviews and ratings are appreciated.

I also would love to see a photo of you reading
Spirituality, Evolution and Awakened Consciousness.

#insightandawareness and tag me @lorraine_nilon

FREE e-book available @ www.Lorraine Nilon.com.au

Take a Moment to Reflect

Contemplation Nurtures your Soul

Also available FREE 12-day emailed Companion Contemplation Course.

Improve your self-reflection skills.

About the Author

Photographed by Paul Mathews

Lorraine Nilon is an Australian writer who lives in regional New South Wales and is a proud mother of twin daughters. She is often found laughing with others about life, and loves nothing more than exploring spirituality and helping others connect with their own truth.

Lorraine is a Soul Intuitive®, Insightful Life Coach, Philosopher and Spiritual Teacher. She has a heightened awareness of the cause and effect of unresolved emotions, and the true nature of who we are hidden beneath our emotional baggage. Lorraine has more than twenty years of experience intuitively reading both conscious and unconscious energy. She explains the complexities and origin of unresolved emotions in a way that is easy for others to understand. Lorraine has a way of igniting your curiosity about yourself and provides a map that assists you to find your own unique path to self-acceptance.

Lorraine is a life researcher who explores the meaningfulness of dealing with the reality of herself as well as sharing what she has learnt, observed, and instinctively knew. She works from the principle that we are all aware of our resonance with truth and yearn to feel reconnected to our own soul truth.

Lorraine has a feet-on-the ground spiritualistic approach to life and expresses the importance of being honest, real, present, and engaged with reality. In her view, it is the only way to truly evolve. She hopes the world is ready to be honest about what we do with our freewill, and encourages others to not bypass the pain of what is stored in their unconsciousness. Lorraine endeavours to be an assistant to clarity so others acknowledge it and free themselves from their oppression.

If you are confused about how you feel and why you do what you do, Lorraine's information provides answers. You may walk in her door, start one of her courses, or pick up one of her books feeling confused and stressed, but you will walk away feeling anchored and more settled with a better understanding of yourself. Regardless of whether you are seeking spiritual enlightenment or just want to feel better about yourself, Lorraine's insightfulness will leave you wanting to know more about your own authenticity. Her books, workshops, online courses, and individual sessions provide opportunities for spiritual growth and soul maturity for those who seek their truth.

Also available for those who want to continue their expedition:

Online courses, workshops, immersive retreats and webinars based on this book.

A guided exploration of all that is featured in Spirituality, Evolution and Awakened Consciousness.

Excellent for those curious souls:

- Who yearn to strengthen their connection with their inner-being.

- Who want to continue to develop a strong relationship with their origins—True Source Divine Origin Consciousness.

- Who would like to explore the beauty of their soul and resolve their own self-opposition.

- Who internally know there is more to them than what they have given themselves credit for.

- Practitioners and nurturers of others who seek to build a greater comprehension.

Free download

Take a Moment to Reflect
Contemplation nurtures your soul

Lorraine Nilon

Take a Moment to Reflect
Contemplation Nurtures Your Soul

As a bonus for purchasing an Insight & Awareness book,
go to Lorraine's website to receive your free e-book copy of
Take a Moment to Reflect

www.lorrainenilon.com.au

Understanding your life experience
and your emotions

Insight &
Awareness

Titles from the Insight and Awareness Anthology

Your Insight and Awareness Book
Your Life is an Expedition to Discover the Truth of Yourself

Breaking Free from the Chains of Silence
A Respectful Exploration into the Ramifications of Abuse Hidden Behind Closed Doors

Take a Moment to Reflect - Quote Booklet
Contemplation Nurtures Your Soul
Free e-book available at www.lorrainenilon.com.au

Energy of Souls
Understanding Your Soul System to Expand
Your Emotional and Spiritual Maturity

Emerging Awareness
An Invitation to Honour the True Essence of Who You Are

Worthy of Recovery
Understanding the Wake Left Behind Life Shocks, Betrayal, Abuse,
Addiction and Narcissistic Relationships

Printed in the USA
CPSIA information can be obtained
at www.ICGtesting.com
LVHW060930070923
757394LV00026B/34